WITH ALL GOD'S PEOPLE

The New Ecumenical Prayer Cycle

Orders of Service

WITH ALL GOD'S PEOPLE

The New Ecumenical Prayer Cycle

Orders of Service

Compiled by John Carden

WCC PUBLICATIONS, GENEVA

Second printing: November 1989

Cover design: Rob Lucas

ISBN 2-8254-0950-2

© 1989 WCC Publications, World Council of Churches,
150 route de Ferney, 1211 Geneva 2, Switzerland

Printed in Switzerland

Contents

Introduction   1

Advent   3

Christmas 14

Epiphany 19

Lent 29

Easter 39

Pentecost 45

The Communion of Saints 54

Thanksgiving for Creation 62

Suffering and Healing in the World 70

Justice and Peace 78

Christian Concern for Human Rights 85

People of Other Faiths 94

Affirmation of Baptism 102

Appendix 114

Index of Music 124

Sources and Acknowledgments 125

Introduction

The following services are included in this volume of the Ecumenical Prayer Cycle in response to requests for material which might be used for meetings of an ecumenical character, either during a particular season of the church's year or in relation to a particular theme.

The services are prototypes only and as such are not final. They are intended to be drawn upon or adapted according to local needs. Indeed, the best reward for the compilers would be for these services to persuade prospective users to draw up their own, and share their results with the rest of us!

The Worship Resource Centre, which is part of the WCC Sub-unit on Renewal and Congregational Life, would gladly receive copies of such acts of worship, and its collection of material from around the world is always available in Geneva for any who are able to visit.

Advent (p. 3)
Christmas (p. 14)
Epiphany (p. 19)
Lent (p. 29)
Easter (p. 39)
Pentecost (p. 45)
Communion of Saints (p. 54)
Thanksgiving for Creation (p. 62)
Suffering and Healing in the World (p. 70)
Justice and Peace (p. 78)
Christian Concern for Human Rights (p. 85)
People of Other Faiths (p. 94)
Affirmation of Baptism (p. 102)

Advent

During the season of Advent the Christian church seeks to identify with countless men and women who, before the birth of Christ, had intimations of his coming; and with all those in the world today who still look for the fulfilment of their expectations.

As a sign of the common heritage which Christians share with the Jewish people a seven-branched candelabrum, or seven candles, may be used as a visual focus for this service.

*   *   *

Hymn

"O come, O come, Immanuel" (*Cantate Domino* No. 53)

or

Taizé
Music: J. Berthier

Wait for the Lord, his day is near.
Nah ist der Herr, es kommt sein Tag.

Wait for the Lord: be strong, take heart!
Nah ist der Herr, habt Mut, seid stark.

Attendez le Seigneur, son jour est proche. Prenez cœur. / Esperad en el Señor, su venida está cerca. Tened coraje. / Aspettate il Signore, il suo giorno è vicino. Abbiate coraggio.

or "We believe, Maranatha!", Francisco F. Feliciano, Philippines (No. 1 in appendix)

The Great Advent Antiphons remind us of humanity's rich expectations of a Redeemer, and look forward to their final fulfilment in the second coming of Jesus.

If candles are being used, one may be lit at each response.

L.   *O Wisdom*, Holy Word of God, who governs all creation with your strong yet tender care; come and show your people the way to salvation.

C.   *Come, Lord Jesus, come.*

L.   *O Sacred Lord* of ancient Israel, who showed yourself to Moses in the burning bush and gave him the holy law in Sinai; come stretch out your mighty hand to set us free.

C.   *Come, Lord Jesus, come.*

L.   *O Flower of Jesse's Stem*, you have been raised up as a sign for all peoples, rulers stand silent in your presence, the nations bow down in worship before you; come quickly to our aid.

C.   *Come, Lord Jesus, come.*

L.   *O Key of David*, and sceptre of the house of Israel, you open and no one can shut, and shut and no one can open; come and free the captive from prison.

C.   *Come, Lord Jesus, come.*

L.   *O Radiant Dawn*, splendour of eternal light, sun of justice; come and shine on those who live in darkness and the shadow of death.

C.   *Come, Lord Jesus, come.*

L.   *O King of all the Nations*, the only joy of every human heart, keystone of the mighty arch of humankind; come and save us whom you fashioned from the dust.

C.   *Come, Lord Jesus, come.*

L.   *O Emmanuel*, king and lawgiver, hope of the nations, saviour of all peoples; come and redeem us, O Lord our God.

C.   *Come, Lord Jesus, come.*

Music: J. Berthier   Taizé.

C.

May be used as an additional response after each petition or after the last one only.

Collect

Almighty God, who spoke in time past in many and various ways to your chosen people by the prophets, and gave us in your Son our Saviour Jesus Christ a fulfilment of the hope of Israel; we pray you to speed the coming of the day when all people shall be subject to him, who lives and reigns with you and the Holy Spirit, ever one God, now and for ever. Amen.

Church of South India, adapted

Psalm

25 or 85

Prophecy

Isaiah 40:1-11 *or* Isaiah 55:6-11 *or* Malachi 3:1-4

Responsory

L.   I wait for the Lord, my soul waits,
        and in his Word I hope.

C.   *In our darkness, there is no darkness with you O Lord,*
        the deepest night is clear as the day.

Music: J. Berthier   Taizé

L.   My soul waits for the Lord
          more than the watchman for the morning.
C.   *In our darkness, there is no darkness with you O Lord,*
          the deepest night is clear as the day.
L.   O Israel, hope in the Lord!
          For with the Lord there is steadfast love,
          and with him is plenteous redemption.
C.   *In our darkness, there is no darkness with you O Lord,*
          the deepest night is clear as the day.
L.   Glory to the Father and to the Son and to the Holy Spirit.
C. _   *In our darkness, there is no darkness with you O Lord,*
          the deepest night is clear as the day.

Gospel

Luke 1:5-23, followed by a short silence

Hymn

Meditation or reading

For suggestions see supplementary material on p. 10.

Magnificat

Cantate Domino No. 62

or Song of Mary with sung refrain

Sanctum nomen...
     My heart praises the Lord;
     my soul is glad because of God, my saviour,
     for he has remembered me, his lowly servant!
     From now on all people will call me happy,
     because of the great things the Mighty God has done for me.
     His name is holy.

Sanctum nomen...
     From one generation to another
     he shows mercy to those who honour him.
     He has stretched out his mighty arm
     and scattered the proud with all their plans.

He has brought down mighty rulers from their thrones,
and lifted up the lowly.
He has filled the hungry with good things,
and sent the rich away with empty hands.

Sanctum nomen...
He has kept the promise he made to our ancestors,
and has come to the help of his servant Israel.
He has remembered to show mercy to Abraham
and to all his descendants for ever.

Glory to the Father, and to the Son and to the Holy Spirit;
as it was in the beginning, is now, and will be for ever.

Sanctum nomen...

Taizé
Music: J. Berthier

Intercession

L.   Remember your Church O Christ; send her continually your Spirit of unity, courage and holiness.

C.   *Always be with us, O Christ*

or Kyrie eleison

Dinah Reindorf, Ghana

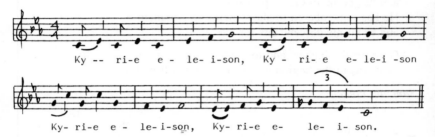

Ky -- ri-e e - le-i-son, Ky - ri - e e- le-i -son

Ky- ri-e e - le-i-son, Ky - ri-e e- le- i- son.

or "Gospodi pomiluj", Kyrie eleison (No. 2 in appendix)

L.   By shedding your blood, you have purified us;
       keep us ready to welcome the Day of your coming.

C.   *Always be with us, O Christ.*

L.   Call from among us bearers of your presence; may they go to the far ends of the earth as tokens of your friendship and signs of your light.

C.   *Always be with us, O Christ.*

L.   Give joy to all your faithful servants; may they follow you all the days of their life.

C.   *Always be with us, O Christ.*

L.   Nurture within us your Spirit of love; may we never close our hearts to any of our sisters and brothers.

C.   *Always be with us, O Christ.*

L.   Bring to an end the divisions between Christians; gather us in one visible communion.

C.   *Always be with us, O Christ.*

L.   Have mercy on all who suffer persecution for your name's sake; uphold them by your strong Spirit, that they may remain true to you in all their trials.

C.   *Always be with us, O Christ.*

L.   Comfort all who are suffering in their hearts or in their bodies; give them health and peace to sing of your power.

C.   *Always be with us, O Christ.*

L.   We pray for all who are leading the nations; give them a sense of what is right, that they may work towards peace and fullness of life for all.

C.   *Always be with us, O Christ.*

L.   Give eternal rest to all who are dying; may the light that never sets shine upon them.

C.   *Always be with us, O Christ.*

Other biddings or prayers may be added, remembering especially those countries prayed for this Advent in the Ecumenical Prayer Cycle.

Almighty God, you have brought us out of the power of darkness into the kingdom of your dear Son; may we wait for his coming in the knowledge that we are in the world but not of the world, since he reigns in your Eternity for ever and ever. Amen.

The Lord's prayer

Hymn

Blessing

L.   Holy, Holy, Holy is the Lord our God,

C.   *Sovereign Ruler of all the world.*

L.   Who was, and is, and is to come.

C.   *Emmanuel. God is with us.*

L.   Let us bless the Lord.

C.   *Thanks be to God.*

The Lord bless you and keep you:
The Lord make his face to shine upon you,
and be gracious to you:
The Lord lift up his countenance upon you,
and give you peace.

The Aaronic blessing, Numbers 6:24-26

Supplementary material

For meditation

A number of readings and meditations suitable for Advent are to be found in:
— *Confessing our Faith around the World: the Caribbean and Central America,* WCC, 1984, notably "There is Light for a Darkened Continent; Message from Latin America", p.80.
— *Immanuel: the Coming of Jesus in Art and the Bible*, Hans-Ruedi Weber, WCC, 1984, notably "The Great Awaiting", p.22.

An Advent meditation from India

Are you a stranger to my country, Lord?
My land of black roots and thick jungles
where the wild boar sharpens his tusks,
where the monkeys chatter in the trees,
and the peacock's shrill note
echoes through the mist-clad hills;
my land of brown, caked river mud
where the elephant and the leopard come to drink,
and the shambling bear with his dreamy eyes
sees the porcupine shedding his quills;
my land with its friezes of palmyra palms
etched sharply against the blue mountains;
my land of low-lying plains
with its miles of murmuring paddy fields
that stretch in undulating waves of green
to the distant horizon;
my land of sapphire skies and flaming sunsets,
my land of leaden grey skies piled high
with banks of monsoon clouds;
my land of stinging rain, of burning heat,
of dark nights, of enchanting moons
that dance behind the coconut fronds;
my land of tanks and pools
where the lazy buffalo wallows
and the red lotuses lie asleep?
No, you are no stranger, Lord,
for the wind whispers of you

and the waters chant your name.
The whole land is hushed in trembling expectancy,
awaiting your touch of creative love.

The Cross is Lifted, Chandran Devanesen

A litany of darkness and light

Voice 1   We wait in the darkness, expectantly, longingly, anxiously, thoughtfully.

Voice 2   The darkness is our friend. In the darkness of the womb, we have all been nurtured and protected. In the darkness of the womb, the Christ-child was made ready for the journey into light.

All   *You are with us, O God, in darkness and in light.*

Voice 1   It is only in the darkness that we can see the splendour of the universe — blankets of stars, the solitary glowings of distant planets.
It was the darkness that allowed the Magi to find the star that guided them to where the Christ-child lay.

All   *You are with us, O God, in darkness and in light.*

Voice 1   In the darkness of night, desert peoples find relief from the cruel relentless heat of the sun.

Voice 2   In the blessed desert darkness Mary and Joseph were able to flee with the infant Jesus to safety in Egypt.

All   *You are with us, O God, in darkness and in light.*

Voice 1   In the darkness of sleep, we are soothed and restored, healed and renewed.

Voice 2   In the darkness of sleep, dreams rise up. God spoke to Jacob and Joseph through dreams. God is speaking still.

All   *You are with us, O God, in darkness and in light.*

Voice 1   In the solitude of darkness, we sometimes remember those who need God's presence in a special way — the sick, the unemployed, the bereaved, the persecuted, the homeless; those who are demoralized and discouraged, those whose fear has turned to cynicism, those whose vulnerability has become bitterness.

Voice 2	Sometimes in the darkness, we remember those who are near to our hearts — colleagues, partners, parents, children, neighbours, friends. We thank God for their presence and ask God to bless and protect them in all that they do — at home, at school, as they travel, as they work, as they play.
All	*You are with us, O God, in darkness and in light.*
Voice 1	Sometimes, in the solitude of darkness, our fears and concerns, our hopes and our visions rise to the surface. We come face to face with ourselves and with the road that lies ahead of us. And in that same darkness, we find companionship for the journey.
Voice 2	In that same darkness, we sometimes allow ourselves to wonder and worry whether the human race is going to survive.
All	*We know you are with us, O God, yet we still await your coming. In the darkness that contains both our hopelessness and our expectancy, we watch for a sign of God's hope.*

Department of Parish Development and Mission, New Zealand

Prayers

I believe with perfect faith in the coming of the Messiah, and even though he tarry, every day I await his coming.

Ani Ma Amin: a song sung by Jews on their way to the
gas chambers during the second world war

Forgive your church, O God, for arrogance and for yielding to racial pride in the persecution of the Jews. Heal the wounding memories of Crusades and Inquisition. Forgive us that we too have been insensitive to the fears and suffering of this people. We have been tolerant of taunts and jibes that insult our fellows and weaken the bonds of our common humanity. We ask your forgiveness for the sake of the greatest Son of Jewry, Jesus the Messiah. Amen.

O God we are in a great darkness.
When we heard of Jesus, we saw a light far off.
Do not let anything put out that light
but lead us nearer to it.

A prayer from Africa

Make us, we beseech you, O Lord our God, watchful in awaiting the coming of your Son, Christ our Lord; that when he shall come and knock, he may find us not sleeping in sin, but awake, and rejoicing in his praises; through the same Jesus Christ our Lord.

Church of South India, collect for Sunday next before Advent

Lord, oil the hinges of our hearts' doors
that they may swing gently and easily to welcome your coming.

Prayer from New Guinea

Lord, may the vision of your future coming shape our present lives, that we may pray today and work today in joyful expectation of tomorrow, ready at all times for our King and Judge.

Lord of our World: Modern Collects from the Gospels, Susan Williams

God of power and mercy, you call us once again to celebrate the coming of your Son. Remove those things which hinder love of you, that when he comes, he may find us waiting in awe and wonder for him who lives and reigns with you and the Holy Spirit, one God, now and for ever.

Anglican Church of Canada, The Book of Alternative Services

Commissioning and benediction

May the blessing of God who risked everything for our sake,
the blessing of the Christ-child who releases in us new visions of hope,
and the blessing of the Holy Spirit who guides and directs us into new forms of obedience, be with us all.

L.   Go forth as preparers and proclaimers.
C.   *We go to make ready for the birth of God in our midst.*
     We go to announce Christ's coming.

L.   The Lord go with you.
C.   *And also with you.*

From New Zealand

Christmas

L.   Lift up your hearts in prayer:
       Lift up your voices in praise.
       Let your eyes rise in expectation,
       And your hands in exultation,
       For the Lord has drawn near,
       And dwells among us.
C.   *We lift them up. Amen.*

Christmas hymn

Poem from India

God of God...
Only the sound of an infant
crying in the night,
a familiar, homely, human sound
like the sound of hooves on flagstones,
like the rattle of chains tethering cattle,
like the crunch of straw in the mouths of oxen,
like the rustle of hay tossed into a manger.

Light of light...
Only the light of a star
falling on an infant in a crib
like the light in a shepherd's lantern,
like the light in the eyes of a mother,
like the light in the learning of wise men,
like the light that lightens each dawn.

Very God of very God...
Only a pillow of straw
and an infant in rags and tatters

like the weather-worn blankets of shepherds,
like dusty, travel-stained garments of travellers,
like old cloths stuffed in a stable window
to keep the draught out and cattle warm.

God is with us,
terribly, simply with us.
And the shadows of men
with arms outstretched to take Him
fall across the manger
in the form of a cross.

The Cross is Lifted, Chandran Devanesen

Christmas carol

Readings

Micah 5:2-4, Matthew 1:18-25, 1 John 1:1-4

Responsory

L. Before the world was created, the Word already existed:
    The Word was with God, and was the same as God.
C. *Gloria in excelsis Deo* (sung)

L. The Word became a human being and, full of grace and truth,
    lived among us.
C. *Gloria in excelsis Deo*

L. We saw his glory, the glory which he received as the Father's
    only Son.
C. *Gloria in excelsis Deo*

L. Glory be to the Father, and to the Son, and to the Holy Spirit.
C. *Gloria in excelsis Deo*

Litany of intercession

Voice   "And this is what will prove it to you; you will find a baby, wrapped in strips of cloth and lying in a manger."

Prayer   Eternal God
we bow before the mystery of your incarnation. You have chosen weakness to confound the strong, and poverty to "send the rich empty away". We remember the millions in our world today who are hungry, who receive no hospitality; all those with whom your Son has become one by being born in a manger.

(silence)

Voice   "Blessed be the Lord our God
C.   *For he has visited and redeemed his people."*

Voice   The angel of the Lord appeared in a dream to Joseph and said, "Herod will be looking for the child in order to kill him. So get up, take the child and his mother and escape to Egypt." Joseph got up, took the child and his mother and left during the night...

Prayer   Merciful God, we call upon you for all who have fled their homes in the darkness of the night... We remember the millions in our world
— who have been made refugees;
— who have sought asylum in lands not their own;
— who are displaced, homeless, landless or lost;
— all whose experience you have made your own in the life of your Son.

(silence)

Voice   "He has stretched out his mighty arm
C.   *and scattered the proud with all their plans."*

Voice   Herod gave orders to kill all the boys in Bethlehem and its neighbourhood who were two years old and younger... In this way what the prophet Jeremiah had said came true:

A sound is heard in Ramah,
the sound of bitter weeping.
Rachel is crying for her children;
she refuses to be comforted,
for they are dead.

Prayer Loving God,
    our hearts are heavy with the sufferings of this world. We remember the many victims of political power and greed:
    — the innocent killed in war and violence;
    — all those who are tortured or put to death;
    — those who languish in prison and camps;
    — those missing or taken hostage;
    — all whose lot your Son shared by being born when Herod was king.

    (silence)

Voice "He has brought down mighty rulers from their thrones,
C. *and lifted up the lowly."*

Voice And Mary said: "I am the Lord's servant;
    may it happen to me as you have said."

Prayer Gracious God, you placed yourself in the care of a woman to show to the world your will to save. Give us grace to follow her example:
    — to become instruments of your grace;
    — servants of your will, and channels of your love.
    May it happen to us as you have willed.

Voice "My soul magnifies the Lord,
C. *and my spirit rejoices in God, my Saviour."*

Prayer O God of Peace, you fill our hearts with hope at every Christmastide for we remember again that this is the world that you have loved. May that hope, peace and joy fill our hearts this night.

C. *Amen.*

Wesley Ariarajah

Our Father

Hymn

(see following page)

Shinsen Sambika
Transl. Hidemi Ito and Sandra Fukunaga

Chugoro Torii

1. The Sun is ris - ing o'er the world To shed its light a - bun - dant; E'en
2. The strength and light of God's own son Brings ev - er - last - ing love; To
3. The Lord who brings sal - va - tion Was born in - to this world. Come,

those who live a - midst the dark Shall find the light comes through. The
all the earth, both great and small, God's won - drous light is shone. He
cel - e - brate, you rich and poor, And share the joy of God. The

Lord, all - know - ing, shares his strength With those a - round the world. The
gives us com - fort, cheer, and might, To share with one an - oth - er. The
Lord who rules the world has come; He guides us ev - 'ry day. Re -

meek, the hum - ble, and the lame, The light of Christ's for you.
weak, the shy, the suf - f'ring crowd, They shall be lift - ed up.
joice and lift your voic - es high, Ho - san - na, Christ our Lord.

Blessing

The blessing of the Lord rest and remain upon all his people,
in every land, of every tongue;
the Lord meet in mercy all that seek him;
the Lord comfort all who suffer and mourn;
the Lord hasten his coming, and give us, his people,
the blessing of peace. Amen.

Epiphany

Now do we celebrate a holy day adorned by three miracles: today a star led the wise men to the manger; today water was made wine at the wedding feast; today Christ vouchsafed to be baptized of John in Jordan that he might save us, Alleluia.

Antiphon of Epiphany Vespers, Western rite

Provision has been made in this service for the commemoration of all three miracles, with a choice of psalm, biblical readings and intercessions to accord with each. In the Orthodox Epiphany, the emphasis is on the baptism of Jesus, and this proposed service draws substantially on worship material from Orthodox sources. In using it, members of small ecumenical groups may appreciate this link with some 130 million Christians in the Eastern and Oriental Orthodox Church families. In an Orthodox setting, the prayers, which in this service come from the Greek and Slavonic side of the family, would be sung. To catch something of the Orthodox atmosphere any well-known icon of the baptism of Jesus would provide an appropriate focus.

* * *

Epiphany hymn

Act of adoration

L.   The Saviour, who is grace and truth, has appeared in the streams of the Jordan, and given light to those that sleep in darkness and shadow. For the Light that no one can approach has come and is made manifest.

C.   *Magnify, O my soul, one of the Trinity*
       who bowed his head and received baptism.

L.   Light from Light, Christ our God has shone upon the world, God made manifest: let all people worship him.

C.   *Magnify, O my soul, one of the Trinity*
      who bowed his head and received baptism.

L.   O Christ, our Master, how shall we your servants give you worthy honour? For you have renewed us all in the waters.

C.   *Magnify, O my soul, one of the Trinity*
      who bowed his head and received baptism.

L.   You, O Saviour, were baptized in Jordan and sanctified the waters: accepting a servant's hand upon your head, you healed the passions of the world. Great is the mystery of your dispensation. Glory to you, O Lord, lover of humankind.

C.   *Magnify, O my soul, one of the Trinity*
      who bowed his head and received baptism.

L.   The true Light has appeared and gives light to all. Christ who is above all purity is baptized with us; he brings sanctification to the water and it becomes a cleansing for our souls.

C.   *Magnify, O my soul, one of the Trinity*
      who bowed his head and received baptism.

L.   That which is outward and visible is earthly, that which is inwardly understood is higher than heaven. Salvation comes through washing, and through water the Spirit: by descending into the water we ascend to God. Glory to you, O Lord; wonderful are your works.

C.   *Magnify, O my soul, one of the Trinity*
      who bowed His head and received baptism.

L.   He who covers the heaven with clouds is himself covered today by the streams of Jordan; and he who takes away the sin of the world is cleansed, that I may be made clean.

C.   *Magnify, O my soul, one of the Trinity*
      who bowed his head and received baptism.

L.   The Only-begotten Son of the Most High Father receives from above the testimony of the consubstantial Spirit. Unto him let us cry aloud: glory to you, O Christ our God, who has made yourself manifest and saved us.

C.   *Magnify, O my soul, one of the Trinity*
      who bowed his head and received baptism.

Orthodox: Patriarch Germanos

Psalm

29 (baptism of Jesus)

> Antiphon: *The voice of the Lord is upon the waters.*
> *May the Lord bless his people with peace.*

or 72 (adoration of the Magi)

> Antiphon: *May the kings fall down before him,*
> *and all nations serve him.*

or 98 (marriage at Cana)

> Antiphon: *Let the floods clap their hands,*
> *let the hills sing together for joy.*

An antiphon is a text, usually taken from the Bible, which is said or sung before or after a psalm or canticle.

Prophecy

Isaiah 55:1-11 (baptism of Jesus), *or* 60:1-6 (adoration of the Magi), *or* 62:1-5 (marriage at Cana)

Responsory

Either

L. Arise shine, for your light has come!
    The glory of the Lord has risen upon you.
C. *Arise, shine, for your light has come!*

L. The Lord rises upon you and his glory appears over you.
C. *The glory of the Lord has risen upon you.*

L. The nations come to your light,
    and kings to the brightness of your rising.
C. *The glory of the Lord has risen upon you.*

L. Lift up your eyes and see,
    they all gather and move towards you.
C. *The glory of the Lord has risen upon you.*

L. People from Sheba will come, bearing gold and incense,
    singing the praise of God.
C. *The glory of the Lord has risen upon you.*

L. Glory to the Father, and the Son and the Holy Spirit.
C. *Arise, shine, for your light has come!*

or

Le Seigneur est ma lumière et mon salut. En lui je me confie.
Der Herr ist mein Licht und mein Heil. Auf ihn vertraue ich.
El Señor es mi luz y mi salvación. En él confío.

Sing both themes simultaneously.

Epistle

Romans 6:3-11

Response

L.   Alleluia
C.   *Alleluia*

L.   With joy you will draw water from the wells of salvation.
C.   *Alleluia*

Gospel

Matthew 3:13-17 (baptism of Jesus), *or* Matthew 2:1-12 (adoration of the Magi), *or* John 2:1-11 (marriage at Cana)

Hymn

This may relate to the chosen gospel reading.

Meditation

Followed by short silence.

Act of praise

The whole or part of this may be used.

May be sung instead of the said response:

Russian Orthodox

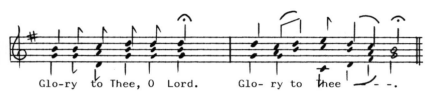

Glo-ry to Thee, O Lord.   Glo- ry to thee - -.

L.   We glorify you, O Master, lover of humankind,
       almighty, pre-eternal King.
       We glorify you, the Creator and Maker of all.
       We glorify you, O only-begotten Son of God,
       born without father from your Mother,
       and without mother from your Father.

C.   *Light from Light, we glorify you.*

L.   In the preceding feast we saw you as a child, while in the
       present we see you full-grown, our God made manifest, perfect
       God from perfect God.
       For today the time of the feast is at hand for us: the choir of
       saints assembles with us and the angels join in keeping festival.

C.   *Light from Light, we glorify you.*

L.   Today the grace of the Holy Spirit in the form of a dove
       descended upon the waters.
       Today the Sun that never sets has risen and the world is filled
       with splendour by the light of the Lord.
       Today the moon shines upon the world with the brightness of its
       rays.
       Today the glittering stars make the inhabited earth fair with the
       radiance of their shining.

C.   *Light from Light, we glorify you.*

L.   Today earth and sea share the joy of the world, and the world is
       filled with gladness.
       The waters saw you, O God, the waters saw you and were
       afraid.

The Jordan turned back, seeing the fire of the Godhead descending bodily and entering its stream.

The Jordan turned back, seeing the Holy Spirit coming down in the form of a dove and flying about you.

C.   *Light from Light, we glorify you.*

L.   The Jordan turned back, seeing the Invisible made visible, the Creator, made flesh, the Master in the form of a servant.

The Jordan turned back and the mountains skipped, looking upon God in the flesh; and the clouds gave voice, marvelling at him who was come, the Light of Light, true God of true God.

C.   *Light from Light, we glorify you.*

L.   For today in the Jordan they saw the triumph of the Master; they saw him drown in the Jordan the death of disobedience, the sting of error, and the chains of hell, and give to the world the baptism of salvation.

C.   *Light from Light, we glorify you.*

Orthodox

Intercession

L.   O Christ, by your epiphany light has shone on us,
        giving us the fullness of salvation:
        grant your light to all we shall encounter today:

C.   *Lord, have mercy.*

Music: J. Berthier   Taizé

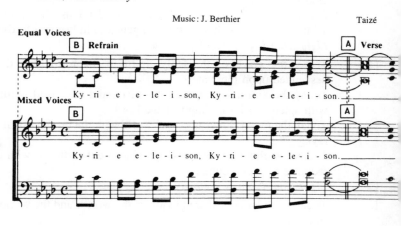

Either

Baptism of Jesus

L.   O Christ, you humbled yourself and received baptism at your
servant's hands, showing us the way of humility:
help us to serve humbly all the days of our life:

C.   *Kyrie eleison.*

L.   O Christ, by your baptism you washed away every impurity,
making us children of God:
grant the grace of adoption to all who are searching for you:

C.   *Kyrie eleison*

L.   O Christ, by your baptism you sanctified creation and opened
the way of repentance to all who are baptized:
make us instruments of your gospel in the world:

C.   *Kyrie eleison.*

L.   O Christ, by your baptism you revealed the Trinity, your Father
calling you his beloved Son, through the Spirit descending upon
you:
renew a heart of worship in the royal priesthood of all the
baptized.

C.   *Kyrie eleison.*

Chaldean Rite

or

Adoration of the Magi

L.   O Christ, whose adoration at the hands of wise men of old
speaks to us of the Spirit's unceasing activity in preparing the
hearts of men and women to receive the good news of the word
of God: renew in your church an eagerness to carry your gospel
to the whole world so that all creatures may adore you, the Lord
of the universe.

C.   *Kyrie eleison.*

or

Marriage at Cana

L.   O Christ, who by your presence at the marriage feast at Cana in
Galilee shared in the joy of men and women; and by your
response to your mother's plea showed forth your glory among

your disciples: give anew to your disciples today a like joy in
your presence, and confidence in the power of common prayer.
C.   *Kyrie eleison.*

The congregation is invited to continue the litany by offering additional
biddings — perhaps linking up the themes of the Epiphany with local
needs and celebrations — to which the response will continue to be: *Kyrie
eleison.*

Collect

Either

*O Lord Jesus Christ, the Only-begotten Son, True God, source of life
and immortality, Light of Light, who came into the world to enlighten
it: shine upon our understanding with your Holy Spirit and accept us
who offer to you glory and thanksgiving for all your great and
wondrous works from all ages, and for your saving grace in these last
times. For you have clothed yourself in our poor and infirm nature,
and submitted yourself to servitude, you who are King of all; and
moreover you have accepted baptism in the Jordan by the hand of a
servant, that having sanctified the nature of the waters, O sinless
Lord, you might lead us to a new birth through water and Spirit, and
restore us again to our original image.*

*For unto you, together with your Father who is without beginning,
and your most holy, good, and life-giving Spirit, are due all glory,
honour, and worship, now, and ever, and unto the ages of ages.
Amen.*

                                                                    Orthodox

or

*O God, who guided by a star the Wise Men to the worship of your Son:
lead to yourself, we pray, the wise and the great in every land, that
unto you every knee may bow, and every thought be brought into
captivity; through Jesus Christ our Lord.*

                                    The Book of Common Worship, Church of South India

Offering

People may then go forward with their offerings, which could be for
local distribution to the needy, or for the work of the worldwide church.
Each receives and lights a candle. A hymn may be sung during the
procession. The following prayers may then be said:

L.   We offer to you, O Ruler of men and women and of heavenly beings, the *gold* of our costly service. Take the labour of our hands, the skill of our minds, the power of our organization. Purge us of pride, and stir us from sloth, that we, being refined by your grace, may become better servants of your kingdom, now and hereafter.

C.   *Amen.*

L.   We offer to you, our Lord and our God, the *incense* of our worship and our prayer. By the gift of your Holy Spirit, you have hung forth a star in the lowly heaven of every Christian soul; grant us with eager feet to follow wherever it leads, until our searching hearts are blessed with the vision of yourself, who are our heaven and our home, for ever.

C.   *Amen.*

L.   We offer to you, O Man of sorrows, the *myrrh* of your church's sufferings. When we have nothing else to give, this offering remains. Where you are on the cross, there also may your servants be. May your perfect sacrifice avail to make our light affliction redemptive in the world, that sharing the fellowship of your sufferings we may rejoice in the power of your resurrection, now and for ever.

C.   *Amen.*

Adapted from an act of offering used on the Eve of Epiphany, 1958,
at the Assembly of the International Missionary Council, Ghana

The Lord's prayer

The blessing

L.   He appeared in human form,
C.   *was shown to be right by the Spirit,*

L.   was seen by angels,
C.   *preached among the nations,*

L.   is believed in throughout the world,
C.   *and taken up in glory.*

L.   God's grace be with you all.
C.   *Amen.*

1 Timothy 3:16 and 6:21

Closing hymn

or

Music: J. Berthier   Taizé

Mixed Voices   *Praise the Lord, all you peoples.*

Lent

In recent years, the commonly held view of Lent as a time of "giving up something" has been replaced by an attempt in many churches to make this a time of special identification with the poor and needy, and with those who in some countries must endure the long involuntary fast of hunger and deprivation. Many ecumenical observances of Lent therefore have focused on simple shared meals, or on days of fasting and prayer which express a sense of solidarity with the hungry. And while such a focus is not precluded in this present suggested act of worship, the emphasis is on the more ancient ecumenical understanding of Lent as a time of contemplating the passion of Jesus — the Christ of the ever-present crosses, to use the words of the 4th-century Egyptian prayer — the better to be prepared to enter with men and women everywhere into the joy of the resurrection which transfigures all situations and circumstances.

* * *

Introductory sentence

Christ himself bore our sins in his body on the tree,
that we might die to sin and live to righteousness.
By his wounds we have been healed.

1 Peter 2:24

Collect

Almighty God, we pray that through this season of Lent, by prayer and study and self-giving, we may penetrate more deeply into the mystery of Christ's sufferings; that following in the way of his cross and passion we may come to share in the glory and triumph of his resurrection; through the same Jesus Christ our Lord. Amen.

Hymn

"Within our darkest night"
or other suitable hymn

Music: J. Berthier   Taizé

Psalm

22:1-8, 11, 14-15, 19, 23-24, to be said responsively

L.   My God, my God why have you abandoned me?
        I have cried desperately for help,
            but still it does not come.

C. *During the day I call to you, my God,*
    but you do not answer;
    I call at night, but get no rest.

L. But you are enthroned as the Holy One,
    the one whom Israel praises.
C. *Our ancestors put their trust in you;*
    they trusted you, and you saved them.

L. They called to you and escaped from danger;
    They trusted you and were not disappointed.
C. *But I am no longer a man; I am a worm,*
    despised and scorned by everyone!

L. All who see me jeer at me;
    they stick out their tongues and shake their heads.
C. *"You relied on the Lord," they say.*
    "Why doesn't he save you?
    If the Lord likes you, why doesn't he help you?"

L. Do not stay away from me!
    Trouble is near, and there is no one to help.
C. *My strength is gone,*
    gone like water spilt on the ground.
    All my bones are out of joint;
    my heart is like melted wax.

L. My throat is as dry as dust,
    and my tongue sticks to the roof of my mouth.
    You have left me for dead in the dust.
C. *O Lord, don't stay away from me!*
    Come quickly to my rescue!

L. "Praise him, you servants of the Lord!
    Honour him, you descendants of Jacob!
    Worship him, you people of Israel!
C. *He does not neglect the poor or ignore their suffering;*
    he does not turn away from them,
    but answers when they call for help."

Response

Music: J. Berthier   Taizé

or

"Chu-yo chu-yo", from Korea (No. 3 in appendix)

Old Testament reading

Exodus 1:8-14, *or* Jeremiah 37:11-16

Response

"O Lord hear my prayer" (sung)

New Testament readings

Mark 14:32-38

Response

Music: J. Berthier
Taizé

Philippians 2:5-11, *or* Hebrews 4:14-5:10

Response

Music: J. Berthier

Taizé

Ky-ri-e, Ky-ri-e, Ky-ri-e e-lei-son lei-son

or

"Senhor, tem piedade de nos", Jaci C. Maraschin, Brazil (No. 4 in appendix)

Meditation

See supplementary material on p. 36 for suggestions

Intercessions

L. Remembering that in his life, passion and death Jesus identified with the poor, the oppressed and the marginalized in society, let us join in a litany of intercession for all for whom Christ suffered and died and for all for whom he lives today:

Voice 1 Let us pray for all who commit themselves to God's mission to establish human relationships based upon freedom and justice.

Voice 2 Save us from indifference and give us courage to work for justice and responsible freedom.

C. *O God of the ever-present crosses, help your servants.*

Voice 1 We pray for the affluent in developed and developing countries that they may not succumb to materialism.

Voice 2 Help us to discover our worth in terms of what we can become as persons rather than in what we own or consume.

C. *O God of the ever-present crosses, help your servants.*

Voice 1	We pray for countries where there is exploitation of natural resources..., where the earth is desecreated to satisfy the lust for profit.
Voice 2	Save us from misusing what you have given for all to share.
C.	*O God of the ever-present crosses, help your servants.*
Voice 1	We pray for all tribal and aboriginal peoples threatened with dispossession and the loss of ancestral lands.
Voice 2	Help us to remember that the land is yours and that we hold it in trust for future generations.
C.	*O God of the ever-present crosses, help your servants.*
Voice 1	We pray for all minority communities faced with the loss of their cultural identity.
Voice 2	Help us to respect each person's way of life.
C.	*O God of the ever-present crosses, help your servants.*
Voice 1	We pray for refugees forcibly uprooted from their homeland to live as aliens in other lands.
Voice 2	Help us to find human solutions to this human tragedy.
C.	*O God of the ever-present crosses, help your servants.*
Voice 1	We pray for all peoples separated from one another because of religious or political differences.
Voice 2	Help us to work for tolerance, dialogue and good will among peoples of differing faiths and political convictions.
C.	*O God of the ever-present crosses, help your servants.*

Adapted from the Worship Handbook of the 7th Assembly
of the Christian Conference of Asia, Bangalore, 1981.
The response is a 4th-century Egyptian prayer

O God, source of love and compassion
in the sufferings of all your children,
we offer our compassion also
for the hungry, and the sick in body, mind or heart,
the depressed and the lonely,
all living in fear and under stress,
all stricken in grief,
the unemployed and the rejected,
and those burning with hatred.

Strengthen us to work for their healing
and inspire us to build with you
the kingdom of love

where none shall cause suffering to others
and all be caring, loving children of yours,
Our compassionate, all-embracing God,
ever present, ever loving,
never failing.

George Appleton, adapted

The Lord's prayer

Hymn

or "Stay with us"

Stay with   us   O   Lord   Jesus Christ: night   will soon

fall.   Then stay   with us   O   Lord   Jesus Christ: light   in   our dark-ness

Benediction

L.   Sisters and brothers,
         let us claim the freedom Christ gives us
         by his self-giving on the cross.
         May he enable us to serve together
         in faith, hope and love.
         Go in peace and serve the Lord.

C.   *Thanks be to God.*

L.   May the God of love who shared his love
          strengthen us in our love for others.
          May the Son who shared his life
          grant us grace that we might share our life.
          And may the Holy Spirit dwelling in us
          empower us to be only and always for others.
C.   *Amen.*

* * *

Supplementary Material

A meditation on Philippians 2:5-11, with bodily movements

"You must work out your own salvation," says St Paul in words which immediately follow his wonderful description of the self-emptying love of God in Christ, which is the subject of one of today's readings. As the Persian proverb puts it: "Blessing is from God, but movement is from humanity." Hence if God's blessing is to be fully enjoyed, it calls for movement from human beings in response.

A sequence of movements which has been found helpful to accompany the slow, contemplative reading of Philippians 2:5-11 proceeds as follows:

"Have this mind among yourselves, which you have in Christ Jesus, who, though he was in the form of God, did not count equality with God a thing to be grasped,...

First, the movement of clenching the fists and letting go again; of screwing up the eyes, and gently opening them again; of tensing the body and relaxing it again, as the words are pondered

... but emptied himself, taking the form of a servant, being born in the likeness of men. And being found in human form...

Pause, and trying to make this more than words, enter into the movement. First standing upright, then slowly bending, kneeling, crouching, becoming little, almost nothing...

Has he not done enough?
But there is deeper humility than that.

*... he humbled himself
and became obedient unto death,
even death on a cross...*

Pause again. This must not just be words. Lie down full length and stretch out your arms sideways, crossways. For you also "have been granted the privilege not only of believing in Christ, but also of suffering for him". (1:29)

*... therefore God has highly
exalted him and bestowed on him
the name which is above every
name, that at the name of Jesus
every knee should bow, in heaven
and on earth and under the earth,
and every tongue confess that
Jesus Christ is Lord, to the glory of
God the Father."*

Now, rising to your feet, stretch your hands upwards...

bow the knee...
rise again...
touch the tongue ...
raise the arms to acknowledge and share in the exaltation of Jesus, his kingship, his ascension, and his glory.

The Declaration on Fasting and Prayer made by Christians in Uruguay concerned with peace and justice takes the subject of prayer and fasting out of a very narrow ecclesiastical context, and contains much to challenge the life-styles of Christians everywhere. It may be found in *Confessing our Faith around the World. IV: South America*, WCC, 1985, p.105.

A meditation

*Keep in mind that you are dust
  and unto dust you shall return.
Indeed Lord, you've given us a transitory world.
A world whose beauty is expressed in huge variety,
  the subtly-altering tints of dawn and dusk,
  the many-hued rhythms of the seasons,
  the criss-crossing ripples on the surface of quiet pools.*

And we? We spend our time trying to carve
   permanent niches for ourselves,
   furnishing desirable long-term residences
   with things which give us value in our own eyes.

Keep in mind that you are dust
   and unto dust you shall return.
The glories of the world around
   escape our notice by and large.
Songbirds' nests are not quoted on the Stock Exchange;
   so root out the hedgerows
   in the name of economic viability.

Where your treasure is,
   there your heart is too.
Keep in mind that you are dust
   and unto dust you shall return.
You wanted to know what it is like
   to live in an impermanent world,
   or why would you have taken flesh like us?
The fragile structures could not hold you,
   yet you stayed within their grasp until your time came.

Breathing forth your Spirit into this world
   you left us to ponder:
"Let not your hearts be troubled,
   I have overcome."
Keep in mind that you are dust
   and unto dust you shall return.

Ash Wednesday, a celebration of realism, Hilda Mary, r.a.,
All Year Round 1987, British Council of Churches

Easter

Easter is everywhere, at all times

The first resurrection appearance of Jesus in the garden, followed by other appearances on the road to Emmaus, by the shores of the Sea of Galilee, and on the Mount of Olives, has led Christians of widely different traditions and cultures to use an open-air setting as a reminder of the universal significance of the resurrection. In many places the first Easter greetings are always exchanged out of doors.

In this service the universal relevance of the resurrection is represented by contributions from different parts of the world. For those who would like to do something out of doors, the story of the Emmaus walk provides a model, and suggests the possibility of members of the congregation meeting up in twos and threes prior to the service and walking to church together; paying attention to the neighbourhood sights and sounds around them, and seeking to relate these to the worship that follows.

It is suggested that the congregation meets outside, or in a church hall or foyer, or other place, for the opening acclamation and greeting before moving into the place of worship.

* * *

L.   Alleluia. Christ is risen.
C.   *Christ is risen indeed. Alleluia*

L.   Alleluia. Christ is risen and the Lord is here.
C.   *Christ is risen and the Spirit is with us. Alleluia*

L.   Alleluia. Christ is risen for God has worked wonders.
C.   *Christ is risen in glory and power forever. Alleluia*

This may be followed by a greeting such as:

L.   The peace of the Lord be always with you.
C.   *And also with you*

The congregation now moves informally into the meeting place singing:

Christ is ri - sen, Al - le - lu - ia! He is ri - sen, Al - le - lu - ia!

Adapted from the Missa Zimbabwe

He is our Saviour — Alleluia.   He's our Saviour — Alleluia.
Let us adore him — Alleluia.   Let's adore him — Alleluia.
He makes us joyful — Alleluia.   He makes us joyful — Alleluia.

or "Aleluya", from Honduras (No. 5 in appendix)

These can be repeated as many times as are necessary until all are seated.

Opening sentence

Choice of three according to the New Testament reading selected.

"While they were talking and discussing together, Jesus himself drew near and went with them" (Luke 24:15).

or

"As they were speaking together, Jesus himself stood among them" (Luke 24:36).

or

"Jesus revealed himself again to the disciples by the Sea of Tiberias" (John 21:1).

Hymn

"Thine be the glory" (*Cantate Domino* No. 93)

A litany of resurrection appearances

In this litany we are reminded of the rich variety of ways in which Christ appeared to his first disciples. The invocatory refrain is an adapted form of one used in the Lord's supper in the liturgy of the Church of South India, and should be said by the congregation as a response to Christ's presence with us now.

L.   O risen Lord, who in your first appearance to Mary was mistaken for the gardener...

C.   *Be present, be present, O Jesus, good High Priest,*
as you were in the midst of your disciples,
and show yourself to us in all our mistakes and uncertainties.

L.   O risen Lord, who appeared to your dejected disciples on the road to Emmaus, and opened to them the scriptures so that their hearts burned within them...

C.   *Be present, be present, O Jesus, good High Priest,*
as you were in the midst of your disciples,
and set our hearts on fire with love for you.

L.   O risen Lord, who gave to your distraught and distracted followers the assurance of healing and forgiveness...

C.   *Be present, be present, O Jesus, good High Priest,*
as you were in the midst of your disciples,
and bring together all Christians in peace and harmony.

L.   O risen Lord, who mindful of the needs of your disciples prepared a meal by the shores of the Sea of Galilee...

C.   *Be present, be present, O Jesus, good High Priest,*
as you were in the midst of your disciples,
and make yourself known to us in all acts of hospitality and sharing.

L.   O risen Lord, who in your final appearance on the Mount of Olives lifted up hands of blessing on all humankind...

C.   *Be present, be present, O Jesus, good High Priest,*
as you were in the midst of your disciples,
and grant that our prayers and praises today may be taken up into yours on behalf of the whole world.

Reading from the Old Testament

Isaiah 55, *or* Isaiah 61:1-4, *or* Ezekiel 37:1-10

Psalm

30, *or* 103, *or* 145:1-13

This may be either sung or said antiphonally.

Reading from the New Testament

Luke 24:13-35, *or* Luke 24:33-53, *or* John 21:1-14

Easter hymn

Intercessions

> *Lord, as you have entered into our life and death, and call us into your
> death and risen life, draw us now, we pray, by the power of your
> Spirit, into an exchange of gifts and needs, joys and sorrows, strength
> and weakness, with your people everywhere; that united we may be
> obedient to your commission, and together enjoy the promise of your
> presence.*

At this point a short period of quiet reflection followed by discussion
could be used to elucidate:
— some of the doubts and fears felt by those first disciples and experienced by many people today;
— thanksgivings and needs drawn from the current week in the Ecumenical Prayer Cycle;
— local needs;
— themes for prayer suggested by the sounds and sights encountered on
   the way to church; for example, for one person the sound of an aircraft
   overhead might suggest a prayer for all travellers, for someone else
   the light in a bedroom window an urge to pray for the sick, or children
   going to bed... etc.
These concerns may be formulated as biddings which can be incorporated
in the following litany, or shared for use in a period of free prayer.

L.   Let us pray for the whole world, for which Jesus lived and died
        and rose again.
        In your mercy —
C.   *Risen Lord, hear our prayer.*

L.   Let us pray for growing unity between the churches.
        In your mercy —
C.   *Risen Lord, hear our prayer.*

L.   Let us pray that this Easter may be a time of reconciliation for all who are estranged or at enmity with each other.
In your mercy —

C.   *Risen Lord, hear our prayer.*

L.   Let us pray for those who live in fear and doubt, that they may be comforted.
In your mercy —

C.   *Risen Lord, hear our prayer.*

L.   We pray that by our words and in our lives we may be pointers to your living presence in the world.
In your mercy —

C.   *Risen Lord, hear our prayer.*

Collect

Risen Lord,
You walk through this earth
using the feet of very imperfect disciples;
may every race and generation take time to
look up and see you,
draw nearer, listen and worship,
and turn to follow you.
C.   Amen.

Prayer from Australia, adapted

Let us conclude our prayers in the words Jesus himself taught us:

The Lord's prayer

An Easter blessing from Jerusalem

May the love of the cross,
the power of the resurrection,
and the presence of the Living Lord,
be with you always.
And the blessing of the Eternal God,
Creator and Sustainer,
Risen Lord and Saviour,
Giver of holiness and love,
be upon you now and evermore.

Hymn

Prayer on departure

L.   As we leave for home, we pray:

O Saviour,
who journeyed with Luke and Cleopas to Emmaus,
journey with your servants who now prepare to travel,
defending them from every evil happening,
for you alone love all humanity
and you alone are almighty.

Prayer before the beginning of a journey;
Kontakion from the Service Books of the Eastern Church

Pentecost

On the 50th day, seven weeks after Easter, the Christian church celebrates the fulfilment of the promises of the Lord Jesus Christ. As Jews celebrate the first fruits of the harvest, Christians celebrate the first fruits of the Spirit and the foundation of the universal church as the new creation. Many Christians observe the Week of Prayer for Christian Unity during the Pentecost season.

The following order of service emphasizes the communion of the Holy Spirit, and the unity and mission of the church.

* * *

Invocation

either Veni Creator, "Come Holy Ghost our souls inspire" (*Cantate Domino* No.100)

or "Wa Emi-mimo", "Come Holy Spirit", as taught by S. Solanke, Nigeria (No. 6 in appendix)

or the quiet singing of

Come, Holy Spirit
Viens, Saint-Esprit
Komm, Heiliger Geist
Ven, Espíritu Santo

Music : J. Berthier   Taizé

Psalm

104:24-30 said responsively with antiphon

All   *Send forth your Spirit, Lord,*
renew the face of the earth.

or

Come, Holy Spirit
Viens, Saint-Esprit
Komm, Heiliger Geist
Ven, Espíritu Santo

Group 1	Lord, you have made so many things.
	How wisely you made them all.
Group 2	The earth is filled with your creatures.
Group 1	There is the ocean, large and wide,
Group 2	Where countless creatures live,
	large and small alike.
Group 1	The ships sail on it, and in it plays Leviathan,
Group 2	The sea monster which you made.
All	*Send forth your Spirit, Lord,*
	renew the face of the earth.
Group 1	All of them depend on you
Group 2	to give them food when they need it.
Group 1	You give it to them, and they eat it;
Group 2	You provide food, and they are satisfied.
All	*Send forth your Spirit, Lord,*
	renew the face of the earth.
Group 1	When you turn away, they are afraid;
Group 2	When you take away their breath, they die
	and go back to the dust from which they came.
Group 1	But when you give them breath, they are created;
Group 2	you give new life to the earth.
All	*Send forth your Spirit, Lord,*
	renew the face of the earth.

Readings

Ezekiel 36:24-28, Romans 8:14-23, Acts 2:1-13 and 41b-47, John 14:15-27 *or* John 20:19-23

Silence

Meditation

See supplementary material on p. 52 for suggestions

Intercessions

from which a selection may be made:

Litanies for unity

I

L.   Praised be God who enables us through
        the Holy Spirit to confess that Jesus Christ is Lord.

Melchior Vulpius 1609

C.   Al - le - lu - ia_____!
        Al - le - lu - ia_____!

        Al - le - lu - ia_____!   Al - le - lu - ia!
        Al - le - lu - ia_____!   Al - le - lu - ia!

L.   There are varieties of gifts but the same Spirit.
C.   *Alleluia* (sung)

L.   There are varieties of service, but the same Lord.
C.   *Alleluia* (sung)

L.   It is the same God working in us all.
C.   *Alleluia* (sung)

L.   To each of us the Spirit gives gifts for the common good.
C.   *Alleluia* (sung)

II

L.   We seek, O God, the gifts of your Spirit:
        the ability to explore the depths of truth, and
        share what we find with each other and with all people...

Terry MacArthur, USA

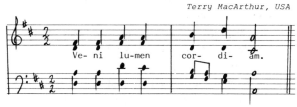

C.   Ve- ni lu-men   cor- di- am.

L.   The gift of faith which undergirds our hope
        and leads us to you...
C.   *Veni Lumen Cordium* (sung)

L.   The resources which give us integrity,
      and heal our divisions...
C.   *Veni Lumen Cordium* (sung)

L.   The power to discern your activity in the world
      and proclaim your presence to those around us
C.   *Veni Lumen Cordium* (sung)

L.   The praise which lifts our spirit and enlivens our worship...
C.   *Veni Lumen Cordium* (sung)

III

L.   Your gifts, O Lord, are ours to share: therefore we pray for
      others.
      For those whose lives of loving faith and service
      have led others to work for reconciliation, we pray:

C.

Version IV   Orthodox liturgy, USSR

Ky - ri - e   e - lei - son,   Ky - ri - e   e - lei - son,

Ky - ri - e   e - le - i - son.

L.   For the sick, the suffering, the captive;
      for their safety and salvation, we pray:
C.   *Kyrie eleison* (sung)

L.   For those who are sent to transmit the gospel
      to people of other continents and religions, we pray:
C.   *Kyrie eleison* (sung)

L.   For all who live and work around the world in the
      spirit of faith, love and hope, we pray:
C.   *Kyrie eleison* (sung)

L.   For the ecumenical movement that it may become a
      pentecostal sign of unity and a creative image of
      God's coming kingdom, we pray:
C.   *Kyrie eleison* (sung)

Adapted from a litany of the Week of Prayer for Christian Unity, 1981

Litany of the Holy Spirit

The response is: *Come into our hearts, make us your new creation*
or *Come, Creator Spirit* (sung)

Spirit of Light, let your wisdom shine on us.

Spirit of Silence: make us aware of God's presence.

Spirit of Courage: dispel the fear in our hearts.

Spirit of Fire: inflame us with Christ's love.

Spirit of Peace: help us be still and listen to God's word.

Spirit of Joy: inspire us to proclaim the good news.

Spirit of Love: help us to open ourselves to the needs of others.

Spirit of Power: give us all your help and strength.

Spirit of Truth: guide us all in the way of Christ.

Michael Shaw and Paul Inwood

Prayer of a young Ghanaian Christian

On your last days on earth
you promised to leave us the Holy Spirit
as our present comforter.
We also know that your Holy Spirit blows over this earth.
But we do not understand him.
Many think he is only wind or a feeling.
Let your Holy Spirit break into our lives.
Let him come like blood into our veins,
so that we will be driven
entirely by your will.
Let your Spirit blow over wealthy Europe and America,
so that people there will be humble.
Let him blow over the poor parts of the world,
so that people there need suffer no more.
Let him blow over Africa,
so that people here may understand what true freedom is.
There are a thousand voices and spirits in this world,
but we want to hear only your voice,
and be open only to your Spirit.

Prayer for the church's mission to the world

O God,
by the power of your Holy Spirit,
set our hearts on fire with a new love for Christ:
that we may work with others to shape the world more nearly to his will;
that we may labour and long for the unity for which he prayed;
that we may be stirred to pray and work for the furtherance of your kingdom,
and that it may be acknowledged with joy to the ends of the earth.
We ask it in his name. Amen.

Prayer used at the Lambeth Conference 1978

Opportunity may be given for a period of free prayer

Collect

O God, of your infinite goodness, set us aflame with that fire of the Spirit Christ brought upon the earth and longed to see ablaze, for he lives and reigns with you and the Spirit now and for ever. Amen.

Prayers from Taizé

The Lord's prayer

Benediction

L.   Let us bless the Lord, alleluia!
C.   *We give our thanks to God, alleluia!*

L.   May the grace of our Lord Jesus Christ,
      the love of God the Father,
      and the communion of the Holy Spirit
      be with us all.
C.   *Amen.*

Hymn

"They'll know we are Christians by our love", words and music by Peter Scholtes

Supplementary Material

Explanation of the third article of the Creed

*I believe
that by my own reason or strength
I cannot believe in Jesus Christ, my Lord, or come to him.
But the Holy Spirit has called me through the gospel,
enlightened me with divine gifts,
and sanctified and preserved me in true faith,
just as he calls, gathers, enlightens, and sanctifies
the whole Christian church on earth
and preserves it in union with Jesus Christ in the one true faith.
In this Christian church God daily and abundantly
forgives all my sins, and the sins of all believers,
and on the last day will raise me and all the dead
and will grant eternal life to me and to all who believe in Christ.
This is most certainly true.*

Small catechism, 1529, in *The Book of Concord:
the Confessions of the Evangelical Lutheran Church,* Philadelphia

"The Unselling of the Pentagon"

C.   *You cannot stop that wind, you cannot kill that fire*
L.   that wind is the wind of truth, that fire is the fire of love
      and that wind keeps right on blowing
      and that fire keeps right on burning.

C.   *You, Caesars of Century One AD,
      you cannot stop that wind, you cannot kill that fire*
L.   all your lying and all your lions cannot stop that wind
      cannot kill that fire
      the truth you sought to cover up is blowing still
      the love you sought to kill is living still.

C.   *And you, Caesars of Century Twenty AD,
      you cannot stop that wind, you cannot kill that fire*
L.   all your lying and all your lawyers cannot stop that wind
      cannot kill that fire
      the truth you seek to cover up is blowing still
      the love you seek to kill is living still.

C.   *You, citizens of Century One AD,
      you cannot stop that wind, you cannot kill that fire*

L.   you can round up followers of the wind and the fire by the hundreds
    you can put them in jail or put them to death

C.   *but you cannot stop that wind, you cannot kill that fire*

L.   that wind gets under your skin, that fire burns into your being
    and that wind stops you and turns you around
    and that fire within bursts into flame.

C.   *And you, citizens of Century Twenty AD,*
    you cannot stop that wind, you cannot kill that fire

L.   you can chant your creeds as you kill each other
    you can flaunt your guns in the face of truth
    but you cannot kill the fire of love
    you cannot stop the wind of truth
    and when you sense your coldness
    and when your fear fills you with emptiness
    that wind will gently breathe new life into your soul
    that fire will fan to life the flame of love.

C.   *And you, spirits of cynicism and despair,*
    you who taunt us and tempt us to say
    humankind is a tragedy, is a meaningless merry-go-round
    you cannot stop that wind, you cannot kill that fire

L.   that fire of faith may flicker and grow dim
    but its embers will burst into flame again and again and again.

C.   *And you, spirits of apathy, fear and unfaith,*
    you who seek to isolate us from our sisters and our brothers
    you who seek to erode our at-one-ment with Life
    you cannot stop that wind, you cannot kill that fire

L.   the persistent gentle breezes of compassion move us towards each other
    the persevering flames of love melt the coldness from our souls.

C.   *And we, brothers and sisters of the here and now,*
    we cannot stop that wind, we cannot kill that fire

L.   that wind is blowing today that fire is burning today
    and when the spirit is low and hope tends to wane
    then you say to me and I'll say to you that wind is
    around that fire is alive

C.   *you cannot stop that wind, you cannot kill that fire.*

Based on the biblical texts "Quench not the Spirit…"
and "The wind bloweth where it listeth…", by Peter Ediger

The Communion of Saints

The Communion of Saints, confessed by all Christians in the Apostle's Creed, is the bond enjoyed by all members of the body of Christ in the Holy Spirit.

Singled out by the church from the beginning until the present time, some members of that body have always been regarded as special models for the Christian life. These include the prophets of the Old Testament, the Blessed Virgin Mary, the first disciples and apostles of Christ, the martyrs and fathers of the early church, as well as that great company of largely unknown Christians whose hidden life and prayer have ever supported the church in its daily combat, and in its faithful proclamation of the gospel.

In the abbey church of Iona, in the Sanctuary movement in the USA, and in the basic communities of Latin America, Christians of very different traditions take comfort and strength from the naming of such witnesses; while in a number of cathedrals special chapels are set aside to commemorate the saints and martyrs of our time, and to intercede for the renewal and unity of the church.

This service, therefore, is proposed for use on any of the many occasions which unite Christians in the commemoration of witnesses past and present. Appropriate occasions would be:

— the Sunday after Pentecost, which is All Saints' day in the Orthodox tradition;

— 1 November, observed as All Saints' day in the Western church;

— on or around the anniversaries of contemporary witnesses and of local saints and martyrs.

* * *

Hymn

(see following page)

Psalm 133, arr. Pablo Sosa

Pablo Sosa, Argentina

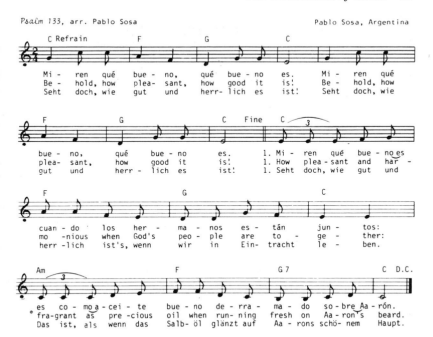

Mi - ren qué bue - no, qué bue - no es. Mi - ren qué
Be - hold, how plea- sant, how good it is! Be - hold, how
Seht doch, wie gut und herr- lich es ist! Seht doch, wie

bue - no, qué bue - no es. 1. Mi - ren qué bue - no es
plea- sant, how good it is! 1. How plea - sant and har -
gut und herr - lich es ist! 1. Seht doch, wie gut und

cuan - do los her - ma - nos es - tán jun - tos:
mo -nious when God's peo - ple are to - ge - ther:
herr -lich ist's, wenn wir in Ein- tracht le - ben.

es co - mo a - cei - te bue - no de - rra - ma - do so - bre Aa - rón.
fra- grant as pre -cious oil when run- ning fresh on Aa - ron's beard.
Das ist, als wenn das Salb- öl glänzt auf Aa - rons schö- nem Haupt.

2. Miren qué bueno es cuando los hermanos están juntos: / se parece al rocío sobre los montes de Sión.

3. Miren qué bueno es cuando los hermanos están juntos, / porque el Señor ahí manda vida eterna y bendición.

2. How pleasant and harmonious when God's people are together: / refreshing as the dew upon the mountain of the Lord.

3. How pleasant and harmonious when God's people are together: / there the Lord God bestows his blessing - life for evermore.

or any other similar hymn

L.   Rejoice in the Lord, you righteous.
C.   *Sing for joy, all upright hearts.*

L.   Heaven, blaze in gladness;
C.   *All saints, apostles, prophets.*

Psalm

92 (sung or said responsively)

Prophecy

Ezekiel 37:1-14 (or 9-14)

Responsory

L.   The good never falter. They are remembered for ever.

C.   *The good never falter. They are remembered for ever.*

L.   Happy are they who fear God, and have great delight in his teaching.

C.   *They are remembered for ever.*

L.   Their children will flourish and prosper, the house of the upright is blessed.

C.   *They are remembered for ever.*

L.   He rises, the Light of the upright, tender, compassionate and good.

C.   *They are remembered for ever.*

L.   Their justice remains for ever, their heads are crowned with glory.

C.   *They are remembered for ever.*

L.   Glory to the Father, and the Son and the Holy Spirit.

C.   *The good never falter. They are remembered for ever.*

Epistle

Hebrews 11:32-12:2 *or* Hebrews 12:22-29 *or* Revelation 19:5-10

L.   Alleluia

C.   *Alleluia* (sung)

Music: J. Berthier   Taizé

or "Vesnica pomenire", "Eternal memory" from the Romanian liturgy (No. 7 in appendix)

L.   You have delivered my soul from death,
             my eyes from tears, my feet from stumbling;
             I walk before the Lord, in the land of the living.

C.   *Alleluia* (sung)

Gospel

Matthew 5:1-12 *or* Matthew 26:6-13

Hymn
or Jesu tawa pano (No. 8 in appendix)

Meditation
followed by a short silence

Litany of praise and intercession
Lord have mercy,
— *Christ have mercy.*

Lord have mercy,
— *Christ hear us.*

God the Father in heaven,
— *Mercy for us!*

God the Son, Redeemer of the world,
— *Mercy for us!*

God the Holy Spirit,
— *Mercy for us!*

God, one God, thrice holy,
— *Mercy for us!*

With the angels, the archangels and the spirits of the blessed,
Lord, we praise you!
— *Glory! Lord of Life!*

With the patriarchs and the prophets, Lord, we bless you!
— *Glory! Lord of Life!*

With the Virgin Mary, Mother of our Saviour, Lord, we magnify you!
— *Glory! Lord of Life!*

With the apostles and the evangelists, Lord, we give you thanks!
— *Glory! Lord of Life!*

With all Christ's martyrs (here mention may be made of local martyrs),
Lord, we offer you our bodies in sacrifice!
— *Glory! Lord of Life!*

With all the saints (here mention may be made of local saints), witnesses
to the gospel, Lord, we consecrate our lives!
— *Glory! Lord of Life!*

With all the faithful of the church, Lord, we adore you!
— *Glory! Lord of Life!*

Father, of your infinite goodness, set us aflame with that fire of the Spirit Christ brought upon earth and longed to see ablaze.

Music: J. Berthier   Taizé

Almighty God, there is no greater love than to give our lives for your friends. Grant us such courage, that in the company of your martyrs we may at last gaze with joy upon the face of Christ, and find in his glory the crown of your eternal life.

— *Kyrie eleison* (sung)

God of all holiness, you manifested your love in such signs of grace, that Mary sang and rejoiced in your Spirit. Grant us such obedient hearts, that we like Mary may believe in your word, and be gladdened by the gift of your Son, Jesus Christ.

— *Kyrie eleison* (sung)

Adaptation of litany of saints, the Taizé Office

A period of free prayer may follow.

L.   Almighty God, break the power of evil, let your glory appear among us and make us sharers of your eternity, with all your saints, through Jesus Christ our Lord.

C.   *Amen.*

The Lord's prayer

Benediction

L.   Happy are you if they persecute you;
C.   *If they slander you because of Christ.*

L.   Be glad and leap for joy;
C.   *For great is your reward in heaven.*

L.   Let us bless the Lord.
C.   *Thanks be to God.*

All   *The grace of our Lord Jesus Christ, the love of God, and the fellowship of the Holy Spirit be with us all now and always. Amen.*

* * *

Supplementary Material

Some acts of commemoration of contemporary witnesses

One very informal service to commemorate the Communion of Saints used in Britain commences with a brief period of discussion naming some of the saints especially dear to those present, and singling out some of the qualities and gifts for which thanks are to be given and intercession made.

We remember, O God, those through whom you have acted, in the world, in the church, and in our own experience. We invoke their names, that they may stand beside us and provide us with the insight of their lives and the encouragement of their prayers:

Great convert Paul, missionary and "man in Christ":
Stand beside us

Little poor woman of Calcutta, Mother Teresa:
Stand beside us.

John, exile on Patmos, with a vision and care for the seven churches of Asia:
Stand beside us.

For the faithful priests and pastors of our earlier years, whose teaching and example brought us here tonight:
Stand beside us.

Victims of Hiroshima, Nagasaki, and of the slaughter of the holy innocents:
Stand beside us.

Doctor and writer, St Luke, who preserved for us the story of Emmaus and of a risen Christ who mysteriously walks with his people:
Stand beside us.

Neighbour, casual acquaintance, brother and sister in Christ, in all that you have been, all that you are, and all that you will be:
Stand beside us.

Sanctuary prayer from USA

(Please respond: "Presente")

We stand with Sojourner Truth and Harriet Tubman who followed the call of their consciences in freeing the slaves through the underground railroad.
Presente

We stand with Rosa Parks who was imprisoned for demanding her right to sit in the front of the bus.
Presente

We stand with Martin Luther King who was imprisoned for non-violent protests against laws of discrimination.
Presente

We stand with Raoul Wallenberg who fought to save the Jews from Nazi death camps.
Presente

We stand with Ita, Maura, Dorothy and Jean who were raped and killed for serving the poor.
Presente

We stand with Oscar Romero who gave his life for defending the rights of the persecuted poor of El Salvador.
Presente

We stand with Ivan Betancourt and companions killed at Olancho, Honduras.
Presente

We stand with all the poor, the persecuted, the disappeared and the refugees of Central America.
Presente

We stand with sanctuary workers all over the world who seek to give shelter to refugees.
Presente

Witnesses for peace

An act of recollection used in the abbey church of Iona, Scotland

Sisters and brothers in Jesus Christ,
Let us call to mind and to be present with us
Those who have lived, worked, spoken and
witnessed for peace in this and other ages.

Jesus Christ, Prince of Peace...
Stand with us now

Paul of Tarsus, Apostle of Peace...
Stand with us now

Stephen the Martyr, first of many...
Stand with us now

At this point people may mention a name or names of those who have inspired them on issues of justice and peace. After stating the name, they say, "Stand with us now". They rise on speaking and others around them who want to be associated with that name, stand also e.g. Francis of Assisi... stand with us now.

After names have been called, the leader will proceed:

All you who have died in war
Since the war to end all wars ...
Stand with us now

All you who tread the path of peace...
Stand with us now

Sisters and brothers in Jesus Christ,
Let us stand in silence.
For the world is worried
And the Prince of Peace is moving towards a cross.

(silence)

Do not be afraid... says Jesus,
I have overcome the world
The peace I give is what the world will never take away.

Thanksgiving for Creation

The celebration of God as Creator, expressed in the first article of the creeds, belongs to the essentials of Christian faith. Thanksgiving for all aspects of creation builds on the tradition of the psalms, and provides an appropriate occasion for an ecumenical act of worship. In the Orthodox tradition the celebration of Epiphany includes thanksgiving for creation. Thanksgiving for harvest or rain can also serve as a starting point for celebrating creation in all its richness. This will fall at different times of the year in different parts of the world. The following order of service is based on material that comes mainly from the Pacific Islands and from Africa.

Locally-known hymns of thanksgiving may be introduced throughout the service, for example before or between the readings, before the confession, or at the beginning and end as alternatives to those suggested.

* * *

Hymn

"Let all the islands rise and sing" (see facing page for verse 1)

2. And when we see the stars at night
the many worlds which cross the sky
the sun and moon which give us light,
we praise our God on high.

3. The children playing on the shore,
the sounds of laughter which we hear
their love increasing more and more,
remind us God is near.

4. The palms which bend towards the sky,
the clouds which hurry to and fro,
the birds which fly both low and high,
give joy to earth below.

5. To God the Father, God the Son,
and God the Spirit, praise be done;
may Christ the Lord upon us pour
the Spirit evermore.

Hymns and Songs for Pacific Gatherings, Tonga

Fijian popular melody

1. Let all the is-lands rise and sing, and to our God their prais-es bring; on strings and drum His might pro-claim, shout the glo-ry of His name.

Refrain

Pa-si - fi-ka, Pa-si - fi-ka, with throb-bing reef and cor-al shore,

Pa-si-fi-ka, Pa-si-fi-ka

for fish and shell and might-y whale, for his gifts our thanks we pour.

Litany of praise

Use of one or the other of these litanies of praise provides an opportunity to identify with Christians in Melanesia or in one part of Africa. Any other more local litany of praise may be substituted.

From the Pacific (Melanesia)

L.   For the earth, and all that is part of it:
C.   *We praise you, Father.*

L.   For rocks, signs of your strength and your steadfast love:
C.   *We praise you, Father.*

L.   For shells, signs of your variety and your joy in creating this world, which you have given to our care:
C.   *We praise you, Father.*

L.   For coconuts and taro,* signs of your providence to us:
C.   *We praise you, Father.*

L.   For the birds, signs of the freedom that is ours when we recognize that we are your children:
C.   *We praise you, Father.*

L.   For the fish of the sea and animals that walk on the land, a reminder to us that the new earth is to be a place where your people live, work and share in peace:
C.   *We praise you, Father.*

L.   For insects, their variety, spontaneity and way of growth, signs of the dying and rising to new life that is the central message to us of your son Jesus:
C.   *We praise you, Father.*

L.   For the similarities of one group of people to another, signs of your desire that there is but one fold, and one shepherd:
C.   *We praise you, Father.*

L.   For the difference between one group of people and another expressed in these islands through the variety of language, tradition, custom, denomination, signs of the challenge of your word and your message to each person:
C.   *We praise you, Father.*

L.   For the people present at this celebration, who by their commitment, readiness to learn and listen, and openness of heart and mind are signs of your readiness to forgive the wrongs we commit against you:
C.   *We praise you, Father.*

From Africa

R 1.   Rejoice in the Lord,
       for he has caused the parched earth to be refreshed,
       and where there was nothing but brownness, hardness, and death, there is now greenness covering the soft earth.
       Where there was death there is now newness of life,
       hope has been restored throughout the land.
C.   *We rejoice in the Lord.*

---

* Taro are kinds of tropical plants, the roots of which are used for food.

R 2.   For the clouds that shelter us from the sun,
for the thunder that shakes the earth,
for the lightning streaking across the sky:

C.   *We thank you, O Lord.*

R 1.   Rejoice in the rain that falls at night,
sinking immediately into the parched earth,
swelling half dried roots and sealing wide cracks.
Rejoice in the cooler nights and the budding flowers,
the shooting trees and the tender green grass.

C.   *We rejoice in the Lord.*

R 2.   For the rain that falls at night
refreshing the earth where it falls:

C.   *We thank you, O Lord.*

R 1.   Rejoice in the big drops that fall at noon-day.
Rejoice in the little streams of water
making their way down hills to the valleys below
to swell the rivers and fill the reservoirs
to supply water for cities and for irrigation.

C.   *We rejoice in the Lord.*

R 2.   For the heavy rains
that fill rivers and lakes:

C.   *We thank you, O Lord.*

R 1.   Rejoice in the activity in the villages
as housewives take hoes and baskets and hurry to the field
to test the responsiveness of the soil
by placing in it seeds of hope and expectation.
Rejoice in those who have already prepared their seedbeds
and now hasten to test the strength of carefully selected seeds.

C.   *We rejoice in the Lord.*

R 2.   For the soil, for rain, for seeds, for tools,
for strength of arms and back,
and for the will to work and a mind to create:

C.   *We thank you, O Lord.*

Readings

Old Testament: Genesis 2:8-15 *or* Deuteronomy 26:1-11
Epistle: Romans 8:18-23
Gospel: Matthew 6:25-34

Litany of confession and intercession from the Pacific

L. Lord in your mercy
forgive us for misusing and abusing the wonderful gifts in nature you have provided for us to use and enjoy.

C. *Lord in your mercy, hear our prayer.*

L. Lord in your mercy
save us from selfish ambitions, greed and love of power.

C. *Lord in your mercy, hear our prayer.*

L. Lord in your mercy
deliver us from lightning and tempest, from plague, pestilence and famine; from battle, murder and from sudden death.

C. *Lord in your mercy, hear our prayer.*

L. Lord in your mercy
help all people to be good stewards of the sea and its resources. Help all people everywhere to acknowledge that you alone have spread out the heavens and rule over the seas, and that the waters are a gift from you.

C. *Lord in your mercy, hear our prayer.*

L. Lord in your mercy
help the scientists and technicians of the world to use their knowledge and skills for the good of humankind and not for destructive purposes. May the countries which produce nuclear energy channel such bounty for the good of all.

C. *Lord in your mercy, hear our prayer.*

Further petitions may be added, using especially material from the appropriate week of the Ecumenical Prayer Cycle.

The Lord's prayer

Offering of gifts

L. What shall we give to the Lord for all his generous gifts?

C. *We shall offer to him gladly our great sacrifice of thanks.*

There is now an opportunity for members of the congregation to come forward bringing gifts, whether of produce or of money, or gifts representative of individual skills, or of creation itself.

Hymn for procession

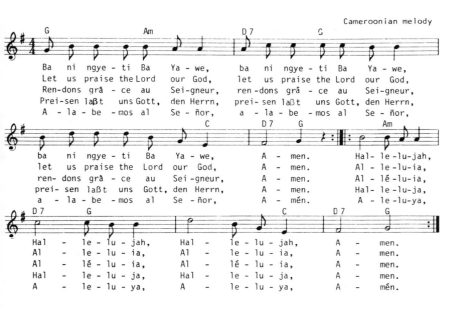

Cameroonian melody

Ba ni ngye - ti Ba Ya - we,
ba ni ngye - ti Ba Ya - we,
Let us praise the Lord our God,
let us praise the Lord our God,
Ren-dons grâ - ce au Sei-gneur,
ren -dons grâ - ce au Sei-gneur,
Prei-sen laßt uns Gott, den Herrn,
prei-sen laßt uns Gott, den Herrn,
A - la - be - mos al Se - ñor,
a - la - be - mos al Se - ñor,

ba ni ngye - ti Ba Ya - we, A - men. Hal- le -lu-jah,
let us praise the Lord our God, A - men. Al - le -lu-ia,
ren- dons grâ - ce au Sei-gneur, A - men. Al - lé-lu-ia,
prei- sen laßt uns Gott, den Herrn, A - men. Hal- le-lu-ja,
a - la - be - mos al Se -ñor, A - men. A - le-lu-ya,

Hal - le - lu - jah, Hal - le - lu - jah, A - men.
Al - le - lu - ia, Al - le - lu - ia, A - men.
Al - lé - lu - ia, Al - lé - lu - ia, A - men.
Hal - le - lu - ja, Hal - le - lu - ja, A - men.
A - le - lu - ya, A - le - lu - ya, A - mén.

L.   Holy Father, our whole life is your gift to us.
Through Jesus you have opened a new way for us to give ourselves to you.
Trusting in him we come with these offerings.

C.   *Lord, accept them and use us in your service,*
For yours is the kingdom, the power and the glory. Amen.

Services for all Seasons, Hyderabad, India

Meditation

Thanksgiving

either Psalm 150

This may be read responsively or used in the way sometimes practised by Christians in the Pacific who describe its use thus:

"This psalm lends itself well to exuberant presentation, and to the use of a variety of musical instruments. The wording below is adapted from the New English Bible. The movements, responses, etc. are suggestions only — congregations should feel free to adapt or substitute as necessary. This rendering calls for a leader to initiate the psalm, and for the participants to be divided into two groups, responding antiphonally to each other. Each group could advance towards the centre while speaking their words, backing up to their places after, while continuing their gestures or sounding of instruments."

L.	O praise the Lord! (extend arms to church)
Group 1	Praise God in this holy place.
Group 2	Praise God in the vault of the heavens, the vault of power (unfold arms to sky).
Group 1	Praise God for mighty works (shouting).
Group 2	Praise God for immeasurable greatness (shouting).
Group 1	Praise God with fanfares on the trumpet (blow horns).
Group 2	Praise God upon lute and harp (strum strings).
Group 1	Praise God with tambourines and dancing (drums and tambourines, twirl around).
Group 2	Praise God with flutes and strings (flutes, pipes, kazoos, same action as group one).
Group 1	Praise God with clash of cymbals (cymbals, if possible or any metallic rhythm).
Group 2	Praise God with triumphal cymbals (all available instruments).
All	*Let everything that has breath praise the Lord!* (all instruments, shouting; everyone advance to centre).
All	*Praise the Lord!* (triumphant shout; gigantic bear hug).

or prayer of thanksgiving from West Africa

Lord of lords, Creator of all things,
God of all things, God over all gods,
God of sun and rain, you created the earth with a thought
and us with your breath.

Lord, we brought in the harvest.
The rain watered the earth,
the sun drew cassava and corn out of the clay.
Your mercy showered blessing after blessing over our lands.

Creeks grew into rivers: swamps became lakes.
Healthy fat cows graze on the green sea of the savanna.
The rain smoothed out the clay walls:
the mosquitoes perished in the high waters.

Lord, the yam* is fat like meat, the cassava* melts on the tongue,
oranges burst in their peels, dazzling and bright.
Lord, nature gives thanks, your creatures give thanks.
Your praise rises in us like the great river.
Lord of lords, Creator, Provider,
we thank you in the name of Jesus Christ.

Dismissal

O God our Creator, by whose mercy and might the world turns safely
into darkness and returns again to light: We give into your hands our
unfinished tasks, our unsolved problems, and our unfulfilled hopes,
knowing that only those things which you bless will prosper. To your
great love and protection we commit each other and all for whom we
have prayed, knowing that you alone are our sure defender, through
Jesus Christ our Lord. Amen.

The Church of South India, adapted

Closing hymn

"Now thank we all our God" (*Cantate Domino* No. 110)

---

*Cassava and yams are edible tubers forming the staple diet in many parts of Africa and the Caribbean.

Suffering and Healing in the World

This service is adapted from one originally prepared by the Christian Medical Commission for use in the chapel in the Ecumenical Centre, Geneva. It seeks to help us to accept, and to live with, the difficult questions; and to use them in a Christian way. The questioning prayer, to which no answer is immediately forthcoming, is a striking feature not only of the prayers of the prophets and psalmists of the Old Testament, and used by our Lord himself, but also of many contemporary prayers in today's suffering and uncertain world.

* * *

Hymn

"Praise to the holiest in the height"

or "There in God's garden stands the Tree of wisdom" (*Cantate Domino* No. 131)

or other suitable hymn

For silent reflection

This life, therefore, is not righteousness but growth in righteousness;
not health but healing;
not being but becoming;
not rest but exercise.
We are not yet what we shall be but we are growing towards it.
The process is not yet finished, but it is going on.
This is not the end, but it is the road.
All does not yet gleam in glory, but all is being purified.

Martin Luther

Prayer for illumination

Give to each of us a candle of the Spirit, O God, as we go down into the deeps of our being. Show us the hidden things, the creatures of our dreams, the storehouse of forgotten memories and hurts. Take us down to the spring of life, and tell each one of us our nature and our name. Give us freedom to grow in order that we may each become that self, the seed of which you planted in us at our making. Out of the deeps we cry to you, O God.

Adapted from a prayer by Jim Cotter, *Prayer at Night*

Psalm

27 (sung or read antiphonally)

Old Testament reading

Habakkuk 1:1-4 and 2:1-4

Responsory

L. O God, help us to be patient towards all that is unsolved in our hearts and in our world.

C. *How long shall we cry for help,*
    and you will not hear?

L. Enable us to accept the questions that confound us.

C. *Why do you countenance oppression...*
    and allow contention and discord to flourish?

L. Give us wisdom so that we do not seek answers that cannot be given.

C. *For the wicked surround the righteous,*
    so justice goes forth perverted.

L. Give us courage to wrestle with such questions in all their perplexity.

C. *We will take our stand to watch,*
    and station ourselves on the tower,
    and look forth to see what you will say to us.

L. Help us to live everything and help us to live it now.

C. *For still the vision awaits its time;*
    it hastens to the end and it will not lie.

L. Grant that we may continue to live in such a manner that we live our way into the ultimate answer.

C. *The vision will surely come, it will not delay...*
    For the righteous shall live by faith.

Short silence

New Testament reading

2 Corinthians 4:7-12 *or* John 9:1-7 (or to verse 41) *or* Luke 22:39-53

Music: J. Berthier   Taizé

My soul reposes in peace on God alone; from him comes my salvation
Bei Gott allein findet meine Seele Frieden; von ihm kommt mir Hilfe
Sólo en Dios descansa en paz mi alma; de él viene mi salvación
L'anima mia si riposa in pace solo in Dio; da lui viene la mia salvezza

Intercessions

Members of the group may be invited to spend some moments in silence reflecting on and writing down the questions they would ask if given an opportunity to meet God face to face. Questions should be formulated under three headings:

— questions about the world;
— questions about one's local community and its needs and problems;
— questions about personal concerns.

Questions may be prompted by the situation in the countries currently being prayed for in the Ecumenical Prayer Cycle.

During the silence, a single large candle should be lit as a symbol of God's presence with us in our wounded and suffering world. To help in preparing questions, the following quotation may be read silently or aloud:

Living the questions of life may be a more realistic and faithful style of Christian living than seeking answers to those questions. All of us are somewhat suspicious of "answers" given to us from any external authority, including the church and the clergy. We are certainly in a time when many traditional "answers" are in question. Questions are more specific and total connections with reality than answers could possibly be.

While we all long for the certainty and security that come with absolute and pat answers, and while we all want to feel that God is in our corner, the reality is that we live by faith and not by certainty or security or even knowledge. Faith implies questioning, searching, wondering and hoping. Faith understands life as a journey that never ends.

Such a quest is not a matter of just having questions, but living the questions we have, and even loving the questions. Somehow, we want to live with our fears and hopes and wonderings in the confidence that, trusting the process in this fashion, we shall live our way into the purpose of God and our own fulfillment.

Living the Questions, Robert A. Raines

The leader then invites members of the group to share in a time of open prayer. Following each question, the person asking it will say:
Lord, in your mercy...
and everyone present will respond: *Hear our prayer*

L.   Let us offer to God our questions about the world....
Lord, in your mercy... Hear our prayer

L.   Let us offer to God our questions concerning our local community....
Lord, in your mercy... Hear our prayer.

L.   Let us offer to God our personal questions and concerns....
Lord, in your mercy... Hear our prayer.

All   *Heavenly Father, we offer you our lives —*
forgive what we have been,
sanctify what we are,
and order what we shall become. Amen.

Hymn

"By gracious powers so wonderfully sheltered" by Dietrich Bonhoeffer (*Cantate Domino* No. 48)

or "Thy kingdom come, O Lord"

N. Zabolotoski

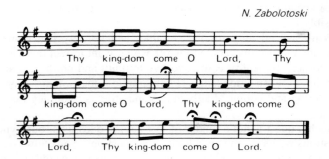

Thy king-dom come O Lord, Thy
king-dom come O Lord, Thy king-dom come O
Lord, Thy king-dom come O Lord.

or other suitable hymn

Litany of assurance

L.   Now faith is the assurance of things hoped for,
      the conviction of things not seen.

C.   *For God so loved the world that he gave his only Son,*
      that whoever believes in him should not perish but have eternal
      life.

L.   What then can we add? If God is for us, who can be against us?

C.   *Who shall separate us from the love of Christ?*
      Shall tribulation, or distress, or persecution,
      or hunger, or danger, or death?

L.   No, in all these things we are more than conquerors
      through him who loved us.

All   *For I am sure that neither death, nor life,*
      nor angels, nor principalities,
      nor things present, nor things to come,
      nor powers, nor height, nor depth,
      nor anything else in all creation,
      will be able to separate us from the love of God
      in Christ Jesus our Lord.

                    Hebrews 11:1; John 3:16; Romans 8:31, 35, 37-39

Hymn

"A safe stronghold our God is still" (*Cantate Domino* No. 146)
or other suitable hymn

Prayer of committal

Into your hands, O God, we commit this your world, this your family,
for which our Lord Jesus Christ was content to be betrayed, and to
suffer death upon the cross. Into your hands we commit all the
problems which seem insoluble, in sure and certain hope; for in you is
our trust. Here and now, we lay all in your hands. All love, all glory,
be unto you, for ever and ever. Amen

Praying for Unity, Edinburgh House Press

* * *

Supplementary Material

Alternative form of intercession

We pray for the whole human family, for your children, our brothers
and sisters, throughout the world. We pray for all who offer to you the
love and worship of their hearts; for men and women of all faiths
believing in you and seeking to serve you, by the light you have
granted to them.

L.   Lord, in your mercy
C.   *Hear our prayer.*

We pray for all Christian people, Catholic, Orthodox, Protestant; for
the peace of your church; for the healing of its schisms; for the unity
for which our Lord Jesus Christ himself prayed.

L.   Lord, in your mercy
C.   *Hear our prayer.*

We pray for the churches to which we belong, and for their healing
ministry.

L.   Lord, in your mercy
C.   *Hear our prayer.*

We pray for all who suffer; for those who are bewildered and perplexed; for the victims of war and violence, of persecution and aggression, of disaster and accident; we pray for the homeless and the hungry; for the destitute and the oppressed; for those who are lonely and unloved; for those who mourn.

L.   Lord, in your mercy
C.   *Hear our prayer.*

We pray for the sick in our own community, in our hospitals and homes; those who turn to us for healing and comfort; those who are known to us; those who have asked for our prayers.

L.   Lord, in your mercy
C.   *Hear our prayer.*

We pray for ourselves and for one another that we may mediate healing and be instruments of your peace and joy; we pray for our own healing and salvation.

L.   Lord, in your mercy
C.   *Hear our prayer*

Adapted from A Service of Healing
as used at St Marylebone Parish Church, London

Prayers

Christians in Tanzania, Uganda and Lebanon who have experienced much privation and suffering in recent times speak of the way in which certain biblical characters and their writings have come alive in their circumstances. Habbakuk and Daniel are two such characters, to whom the following two prayers relate in sharply contrasting style:

Eternal God, who tarriest oft beyond the time we hope for, but not beyond the time appointed by thee; from whom cometh in due season the truth that cannot lie, the counsel that cannot fail: Make us faithful to stand upon our watchtower, and to wait for what thou wilt say to us; that by our faith we may live, and at the last behold thy righteousness prevail; to the glory of thy Name.

From Habakkuk, Eric Milner-White

You are the Lord of fire.
Present in a fiery furnace.
Present in the heat of life.
Present in situations of horror and despair.
Present in the prisons that incarcerate men and women for their beliefs.
Shadrach, Meshach and Abednego were lucky ones, Lord. They came out unscathed.
Not all are so lucky.
Not all withstand the tyrannies of life and remain unharmed.
You are with men and women in their suffering, in their aloneness and ignominy and death.
Be with them.
Be with them through us who are your limbs.
Give even a glimmer of hope in hopeless situations:
for where there is no hope, there is nothing.

Rex Chapman

Justice and Peace

This order of service may be used at any time, particularly:

— on or around 1 January which is observed by many Roman Catholics as a day of prayer for peace;
— during the season of Pentecost;
— on or around 6 August, the Feast of the Transfiguration, which is also the anniversary of the dropping of the atomic bomb over Hiroshima;
— in October during the Week of Prayer for World Peace;
— or on other occasions when prayer for peace and justice seems specially appropriate.

* * *

Hymn

"And every one 'neath the vine and fig tree" (*Vancouver Worship Book* No. 34)

or other suitable hymn

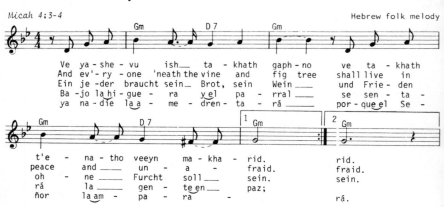

Micah 4:3-4   Hebrew folk melody

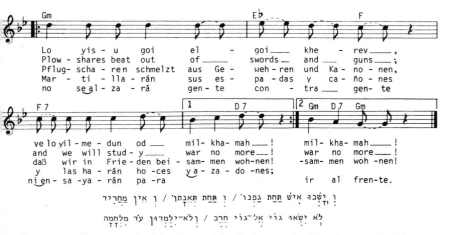

L.   Blessed be the kingdom of the Father, and of the Son, and of the Holy Spirit, now and for always.

C.   *Amen.*

Song of the Beatitudes

from the Russian Orthodox Liturgy (*Cantate Domino* No. 176)

or any sung version of the Beatitudes

Collect

God our Father, you have promised that those who work for peace will be called your daughters and sons. Help us to work without ceasing for that justice which brings true and lasting peace. We ask this through our Lord Jesus Christ.

Roman Missal, Votive Mass for Peace

Old Testament reading

Isaiah 2:1-5

Song

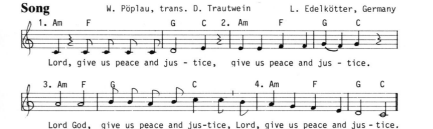

New Testament reading

Matthew 5:1-12

Stand to honour Christ's presence in the gospel

Hymn

"Sing we a song of high revolt" (*Cantate Domino* No. 39)

or any other hymn on the theme of Magnificat

Affirmation of peace and justice

All
: *I believe in God, who is love and who has given the earth to all people.*

  I believe in Jesus Christ, who came to heal us, and to free us from all forms of oppression.

  I believe in the Spirit of God, who works in and through all who are turned towards the truth.

  I believe in the community of faith, which is called to be at the service of all people.

  I believe in God's promise to finally destroy the power of sin in us all, and to establish the kingdom of justice and peace for all humankind.

Group A
: I do not believe in the right of the strongest, nor the force of arms, nor the power of oppression.

Group B
: I believe in human rights, in the solidarity of all people, in the power of non-violence.

A
: I do not believe in racism, in the power that comes from wealth and privilege, or in any established order that enslaves.

B
: I believe that all men and women are equally human, that order based on violence and injustice is not order.

A
: I do not believe that war and hunger are inevitable and peace unattainable.

B
: I believe in the beauty of simplicity, in love with open hands, in peace on earth.

All
: *I do not believe that suffering need be in vain, that death is the end, that the disfigurement of our world is what God intended.*

But I dare to believe, always and in spite of everything, in God's power to transform and transfigure, fulfilling the promise of a new heaven and a new earth where justice and peace will flourish.

Adapted from a creed from Indonesia

Intercessions

This form of intercession uses the traditional spiritual "Kum ba yah" ("Come by here") as a basis. It can be adapted and extended to incorporate many other concerns and biddings: "Someone's lonely... hungry... wounded... singing etc."

All (singing)	*"Someone's crying Lord, Kum ba yah"*
Leader	Someone's crying Lord, somewhere.
	Some is millions, somewhere is many places.
	There are tears of suffering.
	There are tears of weakness and disappointment,
	there are tears of strength and resistance,
	there are the tears of the rich, and the tears of the poor.
C.	*Someone's crying Lord, redeem the times.*

All (singing)	*"Someone's dying Lord, Kum ba yah"*
Leader	Some are dying of hunger and thirst,
	someone is dying because somebody else is enjoying too many unnecessary and superfluous things.
	Someone is dying because people go on exploiting one another.
	Some are dying because there are structures and systems

which crush the poor and alienate the rich.
Someone's dying Lord
because we are still not prepared to take sides,
to make a choice, to be a witness.

C.   *Someone's dying Lord, redeem the times.*

All (singing)   *"Someone's shouting Lord, Kum ba yah"*

Leader   Someone's shouting out loudly and clearly.
Someone has made a choice.
Someone is ready to stand up against the times.
Someone is shouting out,
offering their very existence in love and anger
to fight the death surrounding us,
to wrestle with the evils with which we crucify each
other.

C.   *Someone's shouting Lord, redeem the times.*

All (singing)   *"Someone's praying Lord, Kum ba yah"*

Leader   Someone's praying Lord.
We are praying in tears and anger,
in frustration and weakness,
in strength and endurance.
We are shouting and wrestling,
as Jacob wrestled with the angel,
and was touched,
and was marked
and became a blessing.

We are praying Lord.
Spur our imagination,
sharpen our political will.

Through Jesus Christ you have let us know where you
want us to be.
Help us to be there now,
be with us, touch us, mark us, let us be a blessing,
let your power be present in our weakness.

C.   *Someone's praying Lord, redeem the times.*

All (singing)   *"Someone's praying Lord, Kum ba yah."*

Nairobi Worship Book, 1973-74

Prayer

either

O Lord, our God, creator of heaven and earth,
we thank you and praise you for your love, for your wisdom, for your kindness and mercy.
Make us instruments of love, peace, unity and harmony between people independently of race, colour and creed.
Grant us to respect all of your creation and to look at one another and at all your creatures as brothers and sisters.
Help us to serve one another in humility, simplicity and joy.
Take away from the heart of people the spirit of hatred, violence and rivalry. Amen.

Franciscan prayer, Week of Prayer for World Peace, 1986

or

Grant O Lord that your Holy and life-giving Spirit may so move every human heart, that barriers which divide us may crumble, suspicions disappear and hatred cease; that our divisions being healed, we may live in justice and peace, through Jesus Christ our Lord. Amen.

National Council of Churches in the Philippines

Hymn

"What does the Lord require for praise and offering?"
(music on following page)

1. What does the Lord require
for praise and offering?
What sacrifice desire
or tribute bid you bring?
Do justly; love mercy;
walk humbly with your God.

2. Rulers of earth, give ear!
should you not justice know?
Will God your pleading hear,
while crime and cruelty grow?
Do justly; love mercy:
walk humbly with your God.

3. Still down the ages ring
the prophet's stern commands:
To merchant, worker, king,
he brings God's high demands:
Do justly; love mercy;
walk humbly with your God.

4. How shall our life fulfill
God's law so hard and high?
Let Christ endue our will
with grace to fortify.
Then justly, in mercy,
We'll humbly walk with God.

Albert F. Bayly (1901-84), based on Micah 6:6-8

Sharpthorne   6 6.6 6.3 3.6.   Erik Routley (1917–82)

(Organ)

(Organ)

vv. 1–4   last verse

The peace

L.   O Lord Jesus Christ, who said to your apostles,
    peace I leave with you, my peace I give to you:
    regard not our sins, but the faith of your church,
    and grant it that peace and unity which is agreeable to your will.

C.   *Amen.*

L.   Brothers and sisters, in the love of Christ, let us offer each other
    a sign of peace.

"Salamun, Salamun", "Peace be with you", from Lebanon (No. 9 in
appendix) or other suitable song may be sung

L.   May the Lord of peace give us peace in all ways and at all times.

C.   *Amen.*

Christian Concern
for Human Rights

The Christian concern for human rights is rooted in the conviction that human beings are created in the image of God, and is combined with a realism about the human condition which recognizes its need of restoration and forgiveness.

This order of service may be particularly appropriate:
— on or near 24 October (United Nations Day);
— on or near 10 December (Human Rights Day);
— on or near the anniversary of any who died furthering the cause of human rights;
— in connection with any focus on past or current denials of human rights in a particular country or in respect of a particular people;
— during the days in the church calendar which focus particularly on martyrs e.g. Stephen (26 December), the Innocents (28 December).

* * *

Introductory chant

Ps. 139:12

Music: J. Berthier

Taizé

♩ = 66

La té - | nè - bre n'est point té - | nè - bre de - vant | toi : la

In our dark-ness there is no dark-ness with you O Lord, the

nuit comme le jour est lu - miè — — re. La té-

deep- est night is clear as the day — .

other music of similar mood may be used

This may be sung repeatedly for several minutes as people gather and prepare for worship.

A litany of commandments

The part for the leader may be read by other individual voices. In place of the said response, the following sung response may be used:

All   John Merbecke c. 1550

LÓRD, have mér - cy up - ón us, and in-cline our hearts to keep this láw.

Leader   Our Lord Jesus Christ said, If you love me, keep my
            commandments; happy are those who hear the word of God
            and keep it. Hear then these commandments which God has
            given, and take them to heart.

            I am the Lord, your God: you shall have no other gods but
            me.
            You shall love the Lord your God with all your heart, with
            all your soul, with all your mind and with all your strength.

A.   *Amen. Lord, have mercy.*

L.   You shall not make for yourself any idol.
God is spirit, and those who worship God must worship in spirit and in truth.

A.   *Amen. Lord, have mercy.*

L.   You shall not dishonour the name of the Lord your God.
You shall worship him with awe and reverence.

A.   *Amen. Lord, have mercy.*

L.   Remember the Lord's day and keep it holy.
Christ is risen from the dead: set your minds on things that are above, not on things that are on the earth.

A.   *Amen. Lord, have mercy.*

L.   Honour your father and mother.
Live as servants of God; honour everyone; love the people of God.

A.   *Amen. Lord, have mercy.*

L.   You shall not commit murder.
Be reconciled to your neighbour; overcome evil with good.

A.   *Amen. Lord, have mercy.*

L.   You shall not commit adultery.
Know that your body is a temple of the Holy Spirit.

A.   *Amen. Lord, have mercy.*

L.   You shall not steal.
Be honest in all that you do and care for those in need.

A.   *Amen. Lord, have mercy.*

L.   You shall not be a false witness.
Let everyone speak the truth.

A.   *Amen. Lord, have mercy.*

L.   You shall not covet anything which belongs to your neighbour.
Remember the words of the Lord Jesus: It is more blessed to give than to receive.
Love your neighbour as yourself, for love is the fulfilling of the law.

A.   *Amen. Lord, have mercy.*

The Alternative Service Book 1980. Church of England

or

John Merbecke c. 1550

LORD, have mér-cy up-ón us,   and write all thése thy láws in our héarts,   we be-séech thee.
(both)

Psalms and readings

One or more of the following readings may be used: Genesis 1:26-28, Micah 6:6-8, Luke 4:16-19

Before the readings, or between them, one or more of the following psalms may be said responsively or together: 124; 125; 126; 130:1-6.

Intercessions

These two alternative forms of intercession are prompted by the 30-article Universal Declaration of Human Rights. Agreed by virtually all nations, the Declaration affirms that "all human beings are born free and equal in dignity and rights". A realistic assessment of the human condition suggests that this is not always a present reality, but has yet to be worked and prayed for.

The Declaration continues by asserting that all human beings are entitled "to all the rights and freedoms" set forth, "without distinction of any kind, such as race, colour, sex, language, religion, political or other opinion, national or social origin, property, birth, or other status". It concludes with the affirmation that everyone is entitled to a social and international order in which these rights and freedoms may be fully realized, and it stresses duties and responsibilities which individuals owe to the community. In between are 19 articles which list civil and political rights, and six more which cover economic, social, and cultural rights.

In the prayers which follow, the parts of the leader may be shared by several persons. The following sung responses are suggested, or a spoken response may be used:

Mixed Voices
Taizé
Music: J. Berthier

Ky - ri - e, Ky - ri - e, e - le - i - son.

* Descant ad lib. 2nd time only

or   Music: J. Berthier   Taizé

O Lord hear my pray'r, O Lord hear my pray'r: when I call answer me. O Lord hear my pray'r, O Lord hear my pray'r Come and listen to me. O

or "Doamne Miluieste...", Introit (No. 10 in appendix)

Either

L.   Brothers and sisters, formed in the image of God, let us prayerfully remember before God the human rights solemnly agreed by the nations of this world. Let us give thanks for those places where they exist, and for those persons who have fought and still contend for them. Let us intercede for the conversion of those who deny them, and for the relief of those who are denied them. Let us repent and ask forgiveness for failure to protect and promote them:

The Universal Declaration of Human Rights sets forth:
the right to life, liberty, and security of person;
freedom from slavery and servitude;
freedom from torture;
freedom from cruel, inhuman, or degrading treatment or punishment.

Let us pray for courage and strength for those who contend for these rights, and for relief and salvation for those who are denied them.

C.   *Hear our prayer, O God.*

L.   The Universal Declaration of Human Rights sets forth:
the right to recognition as a person before the law, equal protection of the laws;
the right to an effective judicial remedy;
freedom from arbitrary arrest, detention, or exile;
the right to a fair trial;
the right to a public hearing by an independent and impartial tribunal;
the right to be presumed innocent until proved guilty.

Let us pray for courage and strength for those who contend for these rights, and for relief and salvation for those who are denied them.

C.   *Hear our prayer, O God.*

L.   The Universal Declaration of Human Rights sets forth:
freedom from arbitrary interference with privacy or family;
freedom from arbitrary interference with home or correspondence;
freedom of movement;
the right of asylum;
the right to a nationality.

Let us pray for courage and strength for those who contend for these rights, and for relief and salvation for those who are denied them.

C.   *Hear our prayer, O God.*

L.   The Universal Declaration of Human Rights sets forth:
the right to marry and to found a family;
the right to own property;
freedom of thought, conscience, and religion;

freedom of opinion and expression;
the right of association and of assembly;
the right to take part in government.

Let us pray for courage and strength for those who contend for these rights, and for relief and salvation for those who are denied them.

C.   *Hear our prayer, O God.*

L.   The Universal Declaration of Human Rights sets forth:
the right of equal access to public service;
the right to social security;
the right to work;
the right to rest and leisure;
the right to a standard of living adequate for health and well-being
the right to education;
the right to participate in cultural life.

Let us pray for courage and strength for those who contend for these rights, and for relief and salvation for those who are denied them.

C.   *Hear our prayer, O God.*

or

L.   Brothers and sisters, formed in the image of God,
let us prayerfully remember before God the human rights solemnly agreed by the nations of this world. Let us give thanks for those places where they exist, and for those persons who have fought and still contend for them. Let us intercede for the conversion of those who deny them, and for the relief of those who are denied them. Let us repent and ask forgiveness for failure to protect and promote them.

For those denied a cultural identity, for those whose conscientious objection to military service is not respected, for those denied the right to dissent, for those denied the right to practise their religion or share their faith, let us pray for relief and salvation.

C.   *Have mercy, O God.*

L.   For those who inflict pain or impose burdens, for those who hate or mock, for those who boast or belittle, let us pray for change of heart and life.

C.   *Have mercy, O God.*

L.   For racists and torturers, for those who stereotype or persecute, for those indifferent to evil, for those who live at the expense of others, let us pray for change of heart and life.

C.   *Have mercy, O God.*

L.   For our own country, that its failures and deficiencies in matters of human rights may be speedily corrected and improved, let us pray to the Lord.

C.   *Have mercy, O God.*

L.   For the times we, or any part of the church, have been unfaithful to God's call for freedom, justice, and peace for all, let us repent and ask forgiveness.

C.   *Have mercy, O God.*

Collect

Lord, we are your servants, your chosen ones.
You have called us to serve the cause of right,
to free captives from prison,
and those who live in darkness from the dungeon.
Teach us that this is the fast that pleases you,
to break unjust fetters and to set free the oppressed.
Endow us with your Spirit to bring true justice to the nations,
so that our light may shine in the darkness,
and your light may shine in the sight of men and women everywhere.

A prayer for ourselves as instruments of justice
based on Isaiah 42 and 58

L.   Lord, remember us in your kingdom, and teach us to pray:

The Lord's prayer

Prayer for going forth

O God, send us out into the world in peace.
Help us to hold fast to that which is good.
Help us not to return evil for evil.
Help us to support the faint-hearted.

Help us to uphold the weak.
Help us to honour all people.
O God, help us so to live,
for Jesus' sake. Amen.

Hymn

"Bless and keep us, Lord"

2. Keiner kann allein Segen sich bewahren. / Weil du reichlich gibst, müssen wir nicht sparen. / Segen kann gedeihn, wo wir alles teilen, / schlimmen Schaden heilen, lieben und verzeihn.

3. Frieden gabst du schon, Frieden muß noch werden / wie du ihn versprichst uns zum Wohl auf Erden. / Hilf, daß wir ihn tun, wo wir ihn erspähen - / die mit Tränen säen, werden in ihm ruhn.

4. = 1.

2. Blessing shrivels up when your children hoard it; / help us, Lord, to share, for we can afford it: / blessing only grows in the act of sharing, / in a life of caring, love that heals and glows.

3. Fill your world with peace, such as you intended. / Help us prize the earth, love, replenish, tend it. / Lord, uplift, fulfil all who sow in sadness: / let them reap with gladness, by your kingdom thrilled.

4. = 1.

or

Sursum Corda, F.J. Pagura, Argentina (No. 11 in appendix)

or other suitable hymn

People of Other Faiths

We live in a world where large numbers of people live by other traditions of faith. Recognizing that God is the creator and provider of the whole human family, and respecting all sincere efforts to know and relate to God, this order of worship suggests elements that enable us to pray for neighbours of other faiths.

It may be used on such occasions as the Week of Prayer for World Peace (October) when those of many faiths join in prayers for peace.

* * *

Adoration

L.   The time is coming, indeed it is here, when the true worshippers would worship God in spirit and in truth.

P.   *God is spirit; those who worship him should worship in spirit and in truth.* (John 4:23,24)

      (silence)

L.   This is the place and this is the time;
here and now God waits to break into our experience.

P.   *To change our minds, to change our lives, to change our ways;*

L.   To make us see the world and the whole of life in a new light;

P.   *To fill us with hope, joy, and certainty for the future.*

L.   This is the place, as are all places; this is the time;

P.   *Here and now let us praise God.*

Be Our Freedom Lord, Terry C. Falla

Hymn

"Jesus where can we find you?" (*Vancouver Worship Book* No. 1)

2. Jesus, in hand of the healer
can we feel you there?
Jesus, in word of the preacher
can we hear you there?

3. Jesus, in mind of the leader
can we know you there?
Jesus, in aims of the planner
can we find you there?

4. Jesus, in thought of the artist
can we sense you there?
Jesus, in work of the builder
can we see you there?

(see following page for vv. 5 and 6)

5. Jesus, in face of the famished
can we see you there?
Jesus, in face of the prisoner
can we see you there?

6. Jesus, in faces of children
can we see you there?
Jesus, in all of creation
can we find you there?

or "O praise the Lord", Bhajan melody from India (*Vancouver Worship Book* No. 9)

Psalm

145 or 104:1-15 (read responsively)

Readings

Jonah 4:1-10
Luke 6:37-45 *or* Matthew 8:5-13

Prayer

Eternal God, you are the author of life; all living beings depend on you; you care for all the earth. We pray for our neighbours whose expressions of faith are different from ours; the longings of whose hearts we do not always comprehend. Teach us to know that you love all peoples; help us to respect what we do not yet understand; and to rejoice in the words and acts of truth, beauty and love wherever they may be found. Enable us to love others as you love, and to live with others in ways that build your gracious rule over all of life. We ask this in the name of him who gave himself for all, Jesus Christ, our Lord. Amen.

Responsory

L.　　　Eternal God, free us from fear and prejudice;
　　　　free us from the ignorance that holds us back from rejoicing that we belong to the one human family.
　　　　Set us free to belong and to care.

P.　　　*Lord, set us free.*

L.　　　Loving God, free us from narrowness of mind that is too quick to reject,
　　　　from self-righteousness that is too ready to judge,
　　　　from smallness of spirit that fails to see the good in others.
　　　　Set us free to love and learn.

P.　　　*Lord, set us free.*

L.   Merciful God, free us from our hesitation to witness to your love,
our unwillingness to listen to the witness of others,
our slowness to discern you in places we least expect.
Set us free to perceive and to believe.

P.   *Lord, set us free.*

Litany of gratitude

L.   Let us celebrate our friends and neighbours, men and women whose faith and wisdom have enriched the earth.

(silence)

Seek the truth.

P.   *Listen to the truth.*

L.   Love the truth.

P.   *Serve the truth.*

L.   Teach the truth.

P.   *Live the truth.*

L.   Let us remember with gratitude to God some aspects of the contribution which religions have brought to the lives of the people.

Voice 1   We remember the Jewish people, their life centred in God and God's will. We remember the common heritage of scripture which we share with them.

Voice 2   We remember the rich spiritual traditions of the Hindus; their conviction about the moral laws that rule the universe; the Hindu saints and sages who have dedicated their whole lives in the quest for truth.

Voice 3   We remember Buddhists who follow the Buddha in the path of enlightenment and seek to live a disciplined daily life.

Voice 4   We remember the followers of Confucius and Lao-Tse and their conviction that right relationships between people are the path to wisdom.

Voice 5   We remember Muslims in their total submission to God; in their zeal of devotion and strength of comradeship.

Voice 6   We remember the followers of the religions of Africa; and the Native peoples of the Americas whose religious understanding embraces the whole of life; and all whose religious traditions have enriched the earth and affirmed the sacredness of all creation.

L.   We remember Sikhs, Parsis, and many other religious groups who witness to your unsearchable glory and love. Teach us to discern your presence in the midst of all your people.

Adapted from *New World Liturgy*, Yohan Devananda, Sri Lanka

Intercession

L.   Let us pray for all religious communities and especially for all who teach, preach, instruct and lead; that they may inspire true religion and sincere devotion in the hearts and minds of people.

P.   *Hear our prayer, O God.*

L.   Let us pray for all artists, poets, dramatists, writers and theologians; that they may serve the cause of justice and peace in the interpretation and application of their faiths.

P.   *Hear our prayer, O God.*

L.   Let us pray for the places where there is conflict or war in the name of religion. Let us remember places where there is suspicion or prejudice against any religious community; let us pray for places where there is no religious liberty or the freedom to practise one's own faith.

P.   *Hear our prayer, O God.*

L.   Let us pray for all reformers, for all who seek to correct the wrongs done in the name of religion and its propagation; let us pray for all who work for reconciliation and dialogue, for all who seek to enrich their own faith through their openness to others.

P.   *Hear our prayer, O God.*

Collect

Lord, make us instruments of your peace.
Where there is hatred, let us sow love,
where there is injury, pardon,
where there is doubt, faith,
where there is despair, hope,
where there is sadness, joy.

O Divine Master,
Grant that we may not so much
seek to be consoled as to console,
to be understood as to understand,
to be loved as to love.

For it is in giving that we receive,
it is in pardoning that we are pardoned,
it is in dying that we are born again
to eternal life.

Traditionally by St Francis of Assisi

or sung: "Make me a channel of your peace"

3.O Spir-it, grant that I may nev-er seek so much
to be con-soled as to con-sole,
to be un-der-stood
as to un-der-stand,
to be loved as to love with
all my soul - -

4.Make me a channel of your peace.
   It is in pardoning that we are pardoned,
   in giving to all that we receive,
   and in dying that we're born to eternal life.

Lord's prayer

Benediction

Lead us from death to life,
from falsehood to truth.
Lead us from despair to hope,
from fear to trust,
Lead us from hate to love
from war to peace.
Let peace fill our hearts, our world, our universe.

Prayer for Peace, 1981

Affirmation of Baptism

For Christians of many different traditions Martin Luther's well-known practice, in times of doubt and fear, of recalling the objective fact of his baptism using the words "I have been baptized!" has proved a great source of strength and comfort, and indeed part of their ongoing spirituality. The use of water immediately on entering a church is likewise a reminder to Roman Catholics of a baptism which, though unrepeatable, is nevertheless a cause for continuing thanksgiving, and carries ongoing implications for their life in the body of Christ.

In recent years the practice has grown in many churches of giving their members an opportunity of publicly giving thanks for their baptism, reaffirming their baptismal vows, and seeking God's forgiveness for vows compromised and broken. This service is intended to provide an ecumenical occasion for Christians to remember and to affirm their common basis: the one baptism into the one body of Christ. It is not a repetition of baptism nor a sacramental act, but rather a service of thanksgiving for, and commitment to, the gift of baptism.

The Feast of the Epiphany, the celebration of the Easter Vigil, or any other occasion of renewal or re-dedication are appropriate times for its use.

* * *

Opening hymn

"All people that on earth do dwell" (*Cantate Domino* No. 1)

or "Many are the light-beams"

or other suitable hymn

Anders Frostenson, Sweden   Olle Widestrand, Sweden

1. Man - y   are the   light-beams ___   from the   one   light.   Our   one
1. Strah-len bre-chen   vie - le ___   aus   ei - nem   Licht.   Un - ser
1. Mu -chos res-plan - do - res ___ ,   só -lo u - na   luz: es   la

light   is   Je - sus ___ .   Man - y   are the   light-beams ___
Licht   heißt   Chri - stus ___ .   Strah-len bre -chen vie - le ___
luz   de   Cris - to ___ .   Mu - chos res -plan - do -res ___ ,

from   the   one   light; we   are   one   in   Christ ___ .
aus   ei - nem   Licht- und   wir   sind   eins   durch ihn ___ .
só -lo u - na   luz   que   nos   ha - ce   u - no ___ .

2. Zweige wachsen viele aus einem Stamm. / Unser Stamm heißt Christus. / Zweige wachsen
viele aus einem Stamm -/ und wir sind eins durch ihn.

3. Gaben gibt es viele, Liebe nur eine. / Liebe schenkt uns Christus. / Gaben gibt es viele, Liebe nur eine - / und wir sind eins durch ihn.

4. Dienste leben viele aus einem Geist, / Geist von Jesus Christus. / Dienste leben viele aus einem Geist - / und wir sind eins durch ihn.

5. Glieder sind es viele, doch nur ein Leib. / Wir sind Glieder Christi. / Glieder sind
es viele, doch nur ein Leib - / und wir sind eins durch ihn.

2. Many are the branches of the one tree.
   Our one tree is Jesus.
   Many are the branches of the one tree;
   we are one in Christ.

3. Many are the gifts giv'n, love is all one.
   Love's the gift of Jesus.
   Many are the gifts giv'n, love is all one;
   we are one in Christ.

4. Many ways to serve God, the Spirit is one;
   servant spirit of Jesus.
   Many ways to serve God, the Spirit is one;
   we are one in Christ.

5. Many are the members, the body is one;
   members all of Jesus.
   Many are the members, the body is one;
   we are one in Christ.

Praise

Psalm 107:1-3, 23-32 *or* Ephesians 1:3-14, read responsively

Horatius Bonar 1808-1889   Johann Crüger 1598-1662

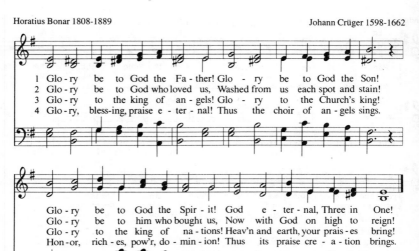

1 Glo-ry   be   to God the Fa - ther! Glo - ry   be   to God the Son!
2 Glo-ry   be   to God who loved us, Washed from us   each spot and stain!
3 Glo-ry   to   the king of an - gels! Glo - ry   to   the Church's king!
4 Glo-ry,   bless-ing, praise e - ter - nal! Thus   the choir of an - gels sings.

Glo - ry   be   to God the Spir - it! God   e - ter - nal, Three in   One!
Glo - ry   be   to him who bought us, Now   with God on high to   reign!
Glo - ry   to   the king of na - tions! Heav'n and earth, your prais - es bring!
Hon - or, rich - es, pow'r, do - min - ion! Thus   its praise cre - a - tion brings.

5 Glory be to God the Father!
  Glory be to God the Son!
  Glory be to God the Spirit!
  God eternal, Three in One!

Confession

L.   Lord, our God, in baptism you have given us a part in the life,
      death and resurrection of Jesus Christ.
      We confess before you that we have not fully lived according to
      the true image of the new humanity. Therefore we cry to you:
C.   *Kyrie eleison.*

Version IV   Orthodox liturgy, USSR

Ky - ri - e   e - lei - son,   Ky - ri - e   e - lei - son,

Ky - ri - e   e - le   -   i - son.

or "A ti, Señor", "O Lord, have mercy", Chilean folk melody (*Vancouver Worship Book* No. 10)

L.   Lord, our God,
        in baptism you have called us to drown day by day our old Adam, that we may rise as new persons in righteousness, justice and holiness.
        We confess before you that we are too lax in striving to realize your will in all realms of life. Therefore we cry to you:
C.   *Kyrie eleison.*
L.   Lord, our God,
        in baptism you have incorporated us into the worldwide body of Christ, so that we may witness before the whole world to your healing and reconciling love.
        We confess before you that we are too lazy in overcoming the divisions between the churches and in making visible our God-given unity within the body of Christ. Therefore we cry to you:
C.   *Kyrie eleison.*
L.   The almighty God, Father, Son and Holy Spirit,
        have mercy upon us,
        forgive us our sins for the sake of Jesus Christ,
        and lead us to renewed and everlasting life
        in the power of the Holy Spirit.
C.   *Amen.*

Collect

Creator Spirit,
who in the beginning hovered over the waters,
who at Jesus' baptism descended in the form of a dove,
who at Pentecost was poured out under the signs of fire and wind,
come to us, open our hearts and minds,
so that we may hear the life-giving word and be renewed by your power
in the unity of the Father and the Son, now and forever. Amen.

Readings

Old Testament: Joshua 24:1,14-16,25: the covenant of Shechem
or Jeremiah 31:31-34: the promise of a new covenant

Response

Version I

Orthodox liturgy, USSR

A - gi - os o The - os,   A - gi - os Is - chi - ros,

A - gi - os __ A - tha - na - tos,   E - le - i - son   i - mas.

Epistle: Ephesians 4:1-6: one God, one faith, one baptism

Gospel: John 3:1-8: the birth of water and spirit
or John 15:1-11: the true vine

Response

Those who have been bap - - tized in Christ,

Ὅ - σοι εἰς Χρι - στὸν ἐ - βα - πτί - σθη - τε
O - si is Chri - ston e - va - pti - sthi - te

have put on Christ for ev - er - more al - le - lu - i - a

Χρι - στὸν ἐ - νε - δύ - σα - σθε ἀλ - λη - λού - ι - α
Chri - ston e - ne - thi - sa - sthe al - li - lu - i - a

Glory to the Father and to the Son and to the Holy Spi - rit

Δό - ξα Πα - τρὶ καὶ Υἱ - ῷ καὶ Ἁ - γί - ῳ Πνεύ - μα - τι καὶ
Tho - xa Pa - tri ke I - o ke A - gi - o Pnev - ma - ti ke

Meditation

Water may now be brought forward and the following meditation used:

L. Water is an element of life and death,
    as streams of water transform desert countries into gardens
    and in the flood life came to an end.
    In the water of baptism we have received
    a part in the life and death of Jesus Christ.
C. *Alleluia* (sung)

Melchior Vulpius 1609

L. Water cleanses us, as the commander Na'aman was cleansed
    from his leprosy in the waters of Jordan.
    By the water of baptism we have been cleansed from our sins by
    forgiveness.
C. *Alleluia*

L.   Without water no life exists on earth, as in the beginning God's life-giving Spirit hovered over the waters.
    In the water of baptism God has given us the life-giving Spirit, who renews us for a new life in holiness and justice.

C.   *Alleluia*

L.   At baptism the name of the triune God was laid upon the baptized.
    Through baptism we were made members of God's worldwide people and called for the royal priesthood of all baptized.

C.   *Alleluia*

L.   The water used at baptism points ahead to the river of the water of life in the New Jerusalem, towards which we move.
    Through baptism we are already, today, integrated into the life of the world to come.

C.   *Alleluia*

Renewal of baptismal vows

L.   Brothers and sisters in Christ:
    In holy baptism God our Lord received you and made you members of Christ's church. Now, therefore, I ask you to renew your baptismal vows: to renounce all the forces of evil, to make public profession of your faith in the triune God, and to commit yourself anew into God's covenant with you.

Renunciation of evil

Either

L.   Remaining under the Lordship of Jesus Christ,
    do you renounce the power of evil?

C.   *Yes, I renounce it.*

L.   Living in the liberty of the children of God,
    do you renounce the rule of the desires of this world,
    the snare of pride, the love of money?

C.   *Yes, I renounce them.*

L.   Witnessing in the world for God's kingdom,
    do you renounce the forces of death, destruction and violence,
    which contradict life under God's will?

C.   *Yes, I renounce them.*

or

L.   Do you reaffirm your renunciation of the forces of evil and death?

C.   *Yes, I do.*

Profession of faith

L.   Now let us confess together our common Christian faith in the words of the *Apostles' Creed*, which in the Western church tradition has been confessed at baptism since the time of the ancient church.

L.   Do you believe in God?

C.   I believe in God, the Father almighty, creator of heaven and earth.

L.   Do you believe in Jesus Christ?

C.   I believe in Jesus Christ, God's only Son, our Lord.
He was conceived by the power of the Holy Spirit
and born of the virgin Mary.
He suffered under Pontius Pilate,
was crucified, died and was buried.
He descended to the dead.
On the third day he rose again.
He ascended into heaven,
and is seated at the right hand of the Father.
He will come again to judge the living and the dead.

L.   Do you believe in the Holy Spirit?

C.   I believe in the Holy Spirit,
the holy catholic church,
the communion of saints,
the forgiveness of sins,
the recurrection of the body,
and the life everlasting. Amen.

L.   This is the faith of the church.

C.   This is our faith.
We believe and trust in one God, Father, Son and Holy Spirit.

Commitment to our baptismal covenant

L.   You have professed faith in God, the Father and Creator: will you work for the integrity of God's creation all over the world?

C.   *Yes, I will.*

L.   You have recognized the one worldwide body of Christ: will you strive to overcome the divisions among Christians and to realize the visible unity of all God's people?

C.   *Yes, I will.*

L.   You have acknowledged a new life in the power of the Holy Spirit: will you engage in promoting justice and peace everywhere in the world?

C.   *Yes, I will.*

L.   May the triune God, Father, Son and Holy Spirit, confirm our human "Yes" with the divine "Amen", and enable us to do what we desire according to God's pleasure.

C.   *Amen* (sung)

Three-fold

Blessing of the water

L.   Lord God almighty, hear the prayers of your people:
we celebrate our creation and redemption.
Hear our prayers and bless this water
which gives fruitfulness to the fields,
and refreshment and cleansing to humanity.
You chose water to show your goodness
when you led your people to freedom through the Red Sea
and satisfied their thirst in the desert with water from the rock.
Water was the symbol used by the prophets
to foretell your new covenant with humanity.

You made the water of baptism holy
by Christ's baptism in the Jordan:
by it you gave us a new birth and renewed us in holiness.
May this water remind us of our baptism
and enable us to share the joy of all who have been baptized,
We ask this through Christ our Lord.

C.   *Amen*

Procession

As a visible expression of our affirmation of baptism, those who wish
are invited to come forward, to put a hand into the water, and perhaps
make the sign of the cross, recalling their baptism.

As an alternative, or in addition, those present are invited to come
forward to light a candle.

During the procession meditative music may be played or hymns sung:

Music: J. Berthier   Taizé

All peoples, praise the Lord!
Louez le Seigneur, tous les peuples!
Lobet alle Völker, lobet den Herrn!
¡Pueblos todos alabad al Señor!

The peace

L.   The peace of the Lord be with you always.

C.   *And also with you.*

L.   As a visible expression of our renewed communion
      let us give each other a sign of reconciliation and peace.

Prayer of intercession

L.   Lord, our God, we ask you for the strength and guidance of the
      Holy Spirit, that we may receive the assurance of our baptism
      and be enabled to live in ways worthy of our gifts and tasks.
      Lord, in your mercy:

C.   *Hear our prayer.*

or: Terry MacArthur, USA

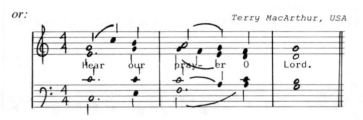

L.   We pray for those not yet baptized
      and for those preparing themselves for baptism,
      that they receive the fullness of your gifts.
      Lord, in your mercy:

C.   *Hear our prayer.*

L.   We pray for those for whom giving or receiving baptism means
      a costly step, and for the hidden Christians who are not allowed
      or who do not dare to live out their baptism, especially in the
      social and political field.
      Lord, in your mercy:

C.   *Hear our prayer.*

L.   We ask you for growing reconciliation, hospitality and recogni-
      tion amongst our churches, in order that your people may
      become more and more a sign of reconciliation and peace for the
      world.
      Lord, in your mercy:

C.   *Hear our prayer.*

L.   We pray for all human beings, your creatures, who thirst for life and who are often close to dying from thirst. Grant them all water of life, Spirit for breathing and hope in you.
Lord, in your mercy:

C.   *Hear our prayer.*

L.   Into your hands, merciful God and Father,
we commend all for whom we pray,
trusting in your mercy now and forever,
through Jesus Christ, your Son, our Lord.

C.   *Amen.*

The Lord's prayer

Blessing

Closing hymn

"We have one Lord" (*Cantate Domino* No. 138)
or other suitable hymn

Appendix

1

Francisco F. Feliciano

2

3

Chu - yo   chu - yo   tu - ro   chu - so - so

Chu - yo   chu - yo   tu - ro   chu - so - so

May your peace shine among us,
may your love set us free,
Lord we pray.

4

Jaci C Maraschin

Se - nhor, tem pie-da — de de nós.   Se -

nhor, tem pie-da — de de nós.   Se -

nhor, tem pie-da - de de nós.

Cris - to, tem pie-da - de de nós.

Cris-to, tem pie-da - de de nós

Cris-to, tem pie-da - de de nós.   Se-

5

ALELUYA

Honduras

A -le - lu- ya, A - le - lu- ya,   A- le - lu -ya, A - le - lu -ya,

A -le - lu - ya, A - le - lu - ya, El Se - ñor re- su - ci - tó.

6

Invocation

in Yoruba, Nigeria
as taught by Samuel Solanke
Para. by I-to Loh

Wa Wa Wa E-mi-mi-mo, Wa Wa Wa A-łag ba-
Come, O Ho-ly Spir-it come, Come, al-might-y Spir-it

E-mi - o-ło-ye
Spir-it of wis - dom

ła Wa - o wa - o wa - o.
come, Come, come, come.

a-łag-ba-ła-me-ła E- mi mi-mo.
al-might-y Tri-ni-ty O Spir-it, come.

* omitted on second time.

7

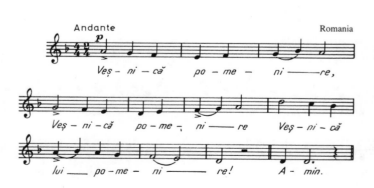

Andante Romania

Veș - ni - că po - me - ni ——re,

Veș - ni - că po - me - ni —— re Veș - ni - că

lui —— po - me - ni —— re! A - min.

8

JESU TAWA PANO (Jesus, we are here)   Patrick Matsikenyiri, Zimbabwe

Je - su ta - wa pa - no, Je - su ta - wa pa - no,

Je - su ta - wa pa - no, ta - wa pa - no mu zi - ta ren - yu.

9

(Peace be with you!)   Lebanon

Sa - la - mun, Sa - la - mun, Sa - la - mun Kul - la - heen!

10

Andantino   Romania

Doam - ne - mi - lu - ieş ——— te, Doam - ne mi - lu -

ieş ——— te, Doam - ne mi - lu - ieş ——— te!

11

Federico J. Pagura (Argentina)   Music: Homero R. Perera (Uruguay-Argentina)

Introducción:

la la la ...

1. Por-

que El ven- ció en la muer-te la con- ju -ra
que El al po - bre le -van-tó del lo -do

— de las ma -lig-nas fuer-zas de la his-
— y re- cha -zó el ha- la -go del di -

to - ria, ____   se - qui- mos no a un
ne - ro, ____   sa - be - mos don-de es-

he- roe ni a un már- tir,   se - gui-mos
tán nues- tras leal- ta - des   y a quien ha-

al Se- ñor de la vic - to- ria.___   Por-
bre-mos

de ser- vir pri- me - ro._____ Por-

que El ha- bló de cruz y la car - ga - ba;

— de sen-da es- tre -cha y la si-guió sin

pau - sa;_____ se -guir sus hue-llas

es nues- tro ca - mi - no; _____ con

El sem-brar-nos: é-sa es nues-tra cau-sa.—

English text on p. 122.
Spanish text on p. 123.

1. Because in death upon the cross he conquered
   the evil forces reigning throughout history,
   we follow not a hero, not a martyr,
   we follow close behind our Lord victorious.

   Because he lifted up all the down-trodden,
   resisting the temptation of possessions.
   We know to whom we'll be forever loyal
   and who it is we'll serve before all others.

   Because he preached the cross and also bore it,
   he spoke of narrow paths and also walked them,
   to follow in his footsteps is our pathway,
   to die and rise with him: that is our calling.

2. Because he preached the kingdom without tiring
   and called us to continue searching for it,
   today among false kingdoms still he calls us,
   to find the one whose reign will last forever.

   Because he is the Lord of earth and heaven,
   of world and life, the end and the beginning,
   because no one can take away his power
   nor can they halt his triumph and his coming.

   So come, all people of this land of beauty
   who've known for years the weight of your oppression,
   now straighten up your backs so nearly broken
   and lift your hearts up to the Lord your Saviour.

3. And all we Christians, all without distinctions,
   all we who take God's name in vain so often,
   now let us go and right our crooked pathways,
   before our laughter changes into crying.

   Because he'll come, by paths that are familiar
   or walking unknown roadways in the darkness,
   the poor and the oppressed will know his justice
   and he'll destroy the powers of sin and evil.

   And in that time the church that has been faithful,
   that gave the world its witnesses and martyrs,
   and did not yield itself before the tyrants,
   nor traded up for gold its sons and daughters.

4. Yes, in that time the church will shine with glory
   that not from gold nor from the sword comes springing,
   but glory that was born upon the dark cross
   that long ago in Golgotha was planted.

   To God the glory, to the Son thanksgiving,
   and praise be given to the Holy Spirit,
   unto the world together let us go now,
   sustained by love and in Christ's hope supported.

1. Porque El venció en la muerte
   la conjura de las malignas fuerzas de la historia,
   seguimos no a un héroe ni a un mártir,
   seguimos al Señor de la Victoria.

   Porque El al pobre levantó del lodo
   y rechazó el halago del dinero,
   sabemos donde están nuestras lealtades
   y a quién habremos de servir primero.

   Porque El habló de cruz y la cargaba;
   de senda estrecha y la siguió sin pausa;
   seguir sus huellas es nuestro camino;
   con El sembrarnos: ésa es nuestra causa.

2. Porque El habló del Reino, sin cansancio,
   y nos llamó a buscarlo una y mil veces;
   debemos hoy entre mil reinos falsos
   buscar el único que permanece.

   Porque El es el Señor del universo,
   principio y fin del mundo y de la vida,
   nada ni nadie usurpará su trono
   ni detendrá su triunfo y su venida.

   Por eso, pueblos de esta tierra hermosa,
   que han conocido siglos de opresiones,
   afirmen sus espaldas agobiadas
   y eleven al Señor sus corazones.

3. Y todos los cristianos, sin distingos,
   que hemos usado en vano el Nombre Santo,
   enderecemos presto los caminos,
   antes que nuestras risas se hagan llanto.

   Porque El vendrá, por sendas conocidas
   o por ocultos rumbos ignorados,
   y hará justicia a pobres y oprimidos
   y destruirá los antros del pecado.

   Y entonces sí, la Iglesia verdadera,
   la que dió santos, mártires, testigos,
   y no inclinó su frente ante tiranos
   ni por monedas entregó a sus hijos.

4. Ha de resplandecer con esa gloria
   que brota no del oro ni la espada
   pero que nace de esa Cruz de siglos
   en el oscuro Gólgota enclavada.

   Al Padre gloria, gratitud al Hijo
   y al Santo Espíritu la alabanza.
   Vayamos hoy al mundo,
   sostenidos por el amor de Cristo y su esperanza.

Index of Music

Adoremus te Domine, 4
Agios o Theos, 106
Alleluia, 47, 56, 107
Aleluya, Aleluya, 117
Amen, Amen, Amen, 110
And ev'ryone 'neath the vine, 78
Ba ni ngyeti Ba Yawe, 67
Because in death upon the cross, 120
Behold, how pleasant, how good it is, 55
Bleib mit deiner Gnade bei uns, 35
Bless and keep us, Lord, 93
Christ is risen, Alleluia, 40
Chuyo chuyo, 115
Come, O Holy Spirit come, 118
Dans nos obscurités, 30
Doamnemiluieste, 119
Gloria, gloria, in excelsis Deo, 15
Glory be to God the Father, 104
Glory to Thee, O Lord, 23
Gospodi pomiluj, 114
Hear our prayer O Lord, 112
In our darkness, 5, 85
Jesus, where can we find you, 95
Jesu tawa pano, 119
Komm, Herr, segne uns, 93
Kum ba yah, my Lord, 81
Kyrie eleison, 8, 24, 48, 58, 104
Kyrie, kyrie, eleison, 89
Kyrie, kyrie, kyrie, eleison, 33
Laudate Dominum, 28
Laudate omnes gentes, 111
Let all the islands rise and sing, 63
Let us praise the Lord our God, 67
Lord, give us peace and justice, 79

Lord, have mercy upon us, 86, 88
The Lord is my light, 22
Make me a channel of your peace, 99
Many are the lightbeams, 103
Miren qué bueno, 55
Mon âme se repose en paix sur Dieu seul, 72
My soul reposes in peace on God alone, 72
O Lord hear my pray'r, 32, 89
Porque El venció en la muerte, 120
Salamun, Salamun, 119
Sanctum nomen Domini magnificat, 7
Senhor, tem piedade de nós, 115
Stay with me remain here with me, 32
Stay with us O Lord Jesus Christ, 35
The Sun is rising o'er the world, 18
Sursum Corda, 120
La ténèbre n'est point ténèbre devant toi, 5, 85
Those who have been baptized in Christ, 106
Thy kingdom come O Lord, 74
Veni lumen cordiam, 47
Veni Sancte Spiritus, 45, 46
Vesnica pomenire, 118
Ve yashevu ish takhath gaphno, 78
Wait for the Lord, 3
Wa Wa Wa Emimimo, 118
We are one in the Spirit, 51
We believe: Maranatha Light of the Day, 114
What does the Lord require, 84
Within our darkest night, 30

Sources and Acknowledgments

We wish to thank all those who have granted permission for the use of prayers, texts and music in this book. We have made every effort to trace and identify them correctly and to secure the necessary permissions for reprinting. If we have erred in any way in the acknowledgments, or have unwittingly infringed any copyright, we apologize sincerely. We would be glad to make the necessary corrections in subsequent editions of this book.

Cantate Domino: an Ecumenical Hymn Book was published on behalf of the World Council of Churches by Bärenreiter-Verlag, Kassel, Federal Republic of Germany, in 1974.

Vancouver Worship Book refers to *Jesus Christ — the Life of the World: a Worship Book for the Sixth Assembly of the World Council of Churches*, published by the WCC, Geneva, in 1983.

Page 3: *Wait for the Lord/Aspettate il Signore/Attendez le Seigneur/Esperad en el Señor/Nah ist der Herr*, composer J. Berthier, "Chants de Taizé", No. 41, 1986 © Ateliers et Presses de Taizé, 71250 Cluny, France.

Page 4: *O Wisdom, Holy Word of God.* Source unknown.

Adoramus te Domine — Gloria, composer J. Berthier, "Canons, litanies et répons de Taizé 2. Chanter le Christ", 1978 © Ateliers et Presses de Taizé, 71250 Cluny, France; also: GIA, Chicago; Collins Lit. Publ., London; Mowbrays, London.

Page 5: *Almighty God, who spoke in time past,* Church of South India, Oxford University Press, Madras. Adapted.

La ténèbre n'est point ténèbre/In our darkness, composer J. Berthier, "Chants de Taizé", No. 10, 1986 © Ateliers et Presses de Taizé, 71250 Cluny, France.

Page 6: *Magnificat,* taken from the Good News Bible.

Page 7: *Sanctum Nomen Domini,* mixed voices, "Music from Taizé", by Jacques Berthier, 1981 GIA Publications, © Ateliers et Presses de Taizé, 71250 Cluny, France; also: GIA, Chicago; Collins Lit. Publ., London; Mowbrays, London.

Page 8: *Kyrie Eleison,* Dinah Reindorf, Ghana.

By shedding your blood, adaptation of pages 34, 51 and 52, from "Praise in all Our Days: Common Prayers at Taizé", 1975. Mowbray's & Co. Ltd., © Cassell Plc, London, UK.

Page 23: *Glory to Thee, O Lord,* Russian Orthodox.
We glorify you, O Master, Orthodox.

Page 24: *Kyrie Eleison 6,* "Music from Taizé", by Jacques Berthier, 1981 GIA Publications, © Ateliers et Presses de Taizé, 71250 Cluny, France; also: GIA, Chicago; Collins Lit. Publ., London; Mowbrays, London.

Page 25: *O Christ, you humbled yourself,* Chaldean Rite.
O Christ, whose adoration at the hands of wise men of old, Orthodox.
O Christ, who by your presence, Orthodox.

Page 26: *O Lord Jesus Christ,* Orthodox.
O God, who guided by a star the wise men, the Book of Common Worship, Church of South India, Oxford University Press, Madras, India.

Page 27: *We offer to you, O Ruler,* adapted from an act of offering used on the eve of Epiphany, 1958, at the Assembly of the International Missionary Council, Ghana.
Blessing, adapted from the Good News Bible.

Page 28: *Laudate Dominum,,* mixed voices, "Music from Taizé", by Jacques Berthier, 1981 GIA Publications, © Ateliers et Presses de Taizé, 71250 Cluny, France; also: GIA, Chicago, Collins Lit. Publ., London; Mowbrays, London.

Page 29: *Almighty God, we pray that through this season of Lent,* in "Contemporary Parish Prayers", Frank Colquhoun, 1975 Hodder & Stoughton, London, UK. Adapted.

Page 30: *Dans nos obscurités/Within our darkest night,* composer J. Berthier, "Chants de Taizé", No. 1, 1986 © Ateliers et Presses de Taizé, 71250 Cluny, France.
My God, my God why have you abandoned me?, Psalm 22, from the Good News Bible.

Page 32: *O Lord hear my prayer,* 4 voices, composer J. Berthier, "Canons, litanies et répons de Taizé 5. Chants Nouveaux", 1982 © Ateliers et Presses de Taizé, 71250 Cluny, France; also: GIA, Chicago; Collins Lit. Publ., London; Mowbrays, London.
Stay with me remain here with me/Bleibet hier und wachet mit mir, composer J. Berthier, 4 Stimmen, "Canons, litanies et répons de Taizé 5. Chants Nouveaux", 1982 © Ateliers et Presses de Taizé, 71250 Cluny, France; also: GIA, Chicago; Collins Lit. Publ., London; Mowbrays, London.

Page 33: *Kyrie, Kyrie eleison,* composer J. Berthier, "Chants de Taizé", No. 10, 1986 © Ateliers at Presses de Taizé, 71250 Cluny, France.
Remembering that in his life, adapted from the Worship Handbook of the 7th Assembly of the Christian Conference of Asia, Bangalore, 1981. The response is a 4th-century Egyptian prayer.

Page 34: *O God, source of love and compassion,* George Appleton, from "One Man's Prayer", SPCK, London, UK. Slightly adapted.

Page 35: *Stay with us/Bleib mit deiner Gnade bei uns, Herr Jesu,* composer J. Berthier, 4 Stimmen, "Canons, litanies et répons de Taizé 5. Chants Nouveaux", 1982 © Ateliers et Presses de Taizé, 71250 Cluny, France; also: GIA, Chicago; Collins Lit. Publ., London; Mowbrays, London.

Sisters and brothers. Source unknown.

Page 36: *A meditation on Philippians 2:5-11 with bodily movements,* Paul Hunt, Church Missionary Society, London, UK.

Page 37: *Keep in mind that you are dust and unto dust you shall return,* "Keep in mind", by Hilda Mary r.a., from "All Year Round 1987" (p.10), British Council of Churches, London, UK.

Page 40: *Christ is risen,* from Missa Zimbabwe. Source untraced.

Page 41: *Be present, be present,* litany of resurrection appearances, adapted from the words in the Church of South India Service of the Lord's Supper, Oxford University Press, Madras, India.

Page 42: *Lord, as you have entered into our life and death.* Source unknown.

Let us pray for the whole world. Source unknown.

Page 43: *Risen Lord, You walk through this earth,* prayer from Australia. Adapted. Source untraced.

May the love of the cross, an Easter blessing from Jerusalem, from "Jerusalem Prayers for the World Today", prayer 95, by George Appleton, SPCK, London, UK.

Page 44: *As we leave for home, we pray,* prayer before the beginning of a journey, Kontakion from the Service Books of the Eastern Church.

Pages 45 and 46: *Veni Sancte Spiritus,* mixed voices, "Canons, litanies et répons de Taizé 3. Chanter l'Esprit", 1978 © Ateliers et Presses de Taizé, 71250 Cluny, France.

Page 46: *Lord, you have made so many things,* Psalm 104:24-30, from the Good News Bible.

Page 47: *Praised be God,* and *We seek, O God,* adapted from a litany of the Week of Prayer for Christian Unity, 1981.

Alleluia, Melchior Vulpius 1609.

Veni Lumen Cordium, by Terry MacArthur, USA, written for "With all God's People".

Page 48: *Your gifts, O Lord,* adapted from a litany of the Week of Prayer for Christian Unity, 1981.

Kyrie eleison, Orthodox liturgy, USSR.

Page 49: *Litany of the Holy Spirit,* 1977 & 1988, Michael Shaw and Paul Inwood. © Published in the UK by St Thomas More Centre, The Burroughs, London NW4 4TY, and in the USA by OCP Publications, 5536 NE Hassalo, Portland, Oregon 07213.

On your last days on earth, "Let your Spirit break in", from "I Lie on My Mat and Pray", Friendship Press, New York, USA.

Page 50: *O God, by the power of your Holy Spirit,* prayer for the church's mission to the world, used at the Lambeth Conference 1978.

O God, of your infinite goodness, collect from "Praise: Prayers from Taizé", 1980, Mowbray's & Co Ltd., © Cassell Plc, London, UK.

Page 51: *They'll know we are Christians by our love,* words and music by Peter Scholtes, has been reprinted with permission of the copyright owner, F.E.L. Publications, 3342 South Sandhill Road, Suite 9-444, Las Vegas, NV 89121-3455, USA. Phone: 702.737-0142. Further reproduction (even words only) is not permitted without F.E.L.'s written permission.

Page 52: *I believe that by my own reason or strength,* explanation of the third article of the creed, reprinted by permission from "The Book of Concord", edited by Theodore G. Tappert, copyright © 1959 Fortress Press, Philadelphia, USA.

"The Unselling of the Pentagon", poem adapted for congregational use by "Sojourners" with the permission of the poet Peter Ediger, from "My People, I am Your Security", reprinted with permission from "Sojourners", Box 2927, Washington DC 20017, USA.

Page 55: *Miren qué bueno,* © music/Spanish/English: Pablo Sosa; German: Burckhardthaus-Laetere Verlag, Offenbach.

Page 56: *The good never falter,* from "Praise in all Our Days: Common Prayers at Taizé" (p.304), 1975. Mowbray's & Co. Ltd., © Cassell Plc, London, UK.

Alleluia, composer J. Berthier, "Chants de Taizé", No. 39, 1986 © Ateliers et Presses de Taizé, 71250 Cluny, France.

Page 57: *Lord have mercy,* from "Praise in all Our Days: Common Prayers at Taizé" (p.307), 1975. Mowbray's & Co. Ltd., © Cassell Plc, London, UK.

Page 58: *Kyrie Eleison 5,* "Music from Taizé", by Jacques Berthier, 1981 GIA Publications, © Ateliers et Presses de Taizé, 71250 Cluny, France; also: GIA, Chicago; Collins Lit. Publ., London; Mowbrays, London.

Almighty God, there is no greater love, adaptation of litany of saints, the Taizé Office. Mowbray's & Co. Ltd. © Cassell Plc, London, UK.

Page 59: *We remember, O God.* Source unknown.

Page 60: *Sanctuary prayer from USA.* Source unknown.

Page 61: *Sisters and brothers in Jesus Christ,* witnesses for peace, act of recollection, "Iona Community Worship Book", used by permission, © Iona Community — Wild Goose Publications, Glasgow, Scotland.

Page 62: *Let all the islands rise and sing,* "Hymns and Songs for Pacific Gatherings". Source untraced.

Page 63: *Litany of praise from the Pacific,* Melanesia. Source untraced.

Page 64: *Litany of praise from Africa.* Source unknown.

Page 66: *Litany of confession and intercession from the Pacific,* Jabez L. Bryce, Fiji.

What shall we give... the power and the glory, versicles and responses for the offering from "Services for all Seasons", Hyderabad, India.

Page 67: *Bani ngyeti Ba Yawe,* text original mungaka; French: Bayiga Bayiga; German: Irmhild Lyonga/Burckhardthaus-Laetere Verlag, Offenbach; Spanish: Pablo Sosa; in "Jesus Christ — the Life of the World: a Worship Book for the Sixth Assembly of the World Council of Churches", 1983 WCC, Geneva, Switzerland.

Page 68: *Lord of lords, Creator of all things,* prayer of thanksgiving from West Africa. Source untraced.

Page 69: *O God our Creator, by whose mercy and might,* Church of South India, Oxford University Press, Madras, India. Adapted.

Page 70: *This life, therefore, is not righteousness,* Martin Luther. Source untraced.

Give to each of us a candle of the Spirit, adapted from a prayer by Jim Cotter, from "Prayers at Night", Cairns Publications, an adapation of a prayer of George Appleton, from "One Man's Prayers" (p.13), SPCK, London, UK.

Page 71: *O God, help us to be patient,* adapted from a meditation inspired by R.M. Rilke, used in "Cairns for a Journey", in Jim Cotter, "Prayers at Night", 1988 3rd edition Cairns Publications, Sheffield, UK. Used with permission.

Page 72: *Mon âme se repose en paix sur Dieu seul,* composer J. Berthier, 4 voix, "Canons, litanies et répons de Taizé 5. Chants Nouveaux", 1982 © Ateliers et Presses de Taizé, 71250 Cluny, France; also: GIA, Chicago; Collins Lit. Publ., London; Mowbrays, London.

Page 73: *Living the questions of life,* from "Living the Questions", by Robert A. Raines, © 1976 Word Incorporated, Waco, Texas, USA.

Page 74: *Thy kingdom come, O Lord,* words and music by N. Zabolotski, "The Kingdom on its Way" (p.56), Risk Book Series No. 10, 1980 © WCC Publications, Geneva, Switzerland.

Page 75: *Into your hands,* "Praying for Unity", Edinburgh House Press, Scotland.

Alternative form of intercession, adapted from a service of healing composed by Christopher Hamel Cooke, for use at St Marylebone Parish Church, London, UK.

Page 76: *Eternal God, who tarriest oft,* from "Habakkuk", published in "Daily Prayer" (p.11), by Eric Milner-White and G.W. Briggs, 1941 Oxford University Press, London, UK. Used with permission.

Page 77: *You are the Lord of fire,* Rex Chapman. Source untraced.

Page 78: *And ev'ryone 'neath the vine and fig tree,* text: Hebrew from Micah 4. English: Dieter Trautwein; German: Friedrich Karl Barth, D. Trautwein; Spanish: Pablo Sosa; © English and German: Burckhardthaus-Laetere Verlag, Offenbach. Used with permission.

Page 79: *God our Father,* Roman Missal, Votive Mass for Peace.

Lord, give us peace and justice, words W. Pöplau, transl. Burckhardthaus-Laetere Verlag, Offenbach; music L. Edelkötter.

Page 80: *Affirmation of peace and justice,* adapted from a creed from Indonesia. Source untraced.

Page 81: *Kumba yah,* from "Africa Sings", Asempa Publishers, Accra, Ghana, by permission from the Department of Faith and Selfhood of the Church, AACC, Lome, Togo.

Page 83: *O Lord, our God, creator of heaven and earth,* Franciscan prayer, Week of Prayer for World Peace 1986, London, UK.

Grant O Lord that your Holy and Life-giving Spirit, from the Philippine Episcopal Church National Commission on Social Justice and Human Rights, published in "Liturgies and Worship Guides" (p.24), 1986 National Council of Churches in the Philippines, Quezon City.

What does the Lord require, words by Albert F. Bayly (1901–84), music by Erik Routley (1917–82) (Sharpthorne 6 6.6 6.3 3.6 HHT 99), 1988 "Hymns Ancient and Modern, New Standard", © music world rights Oxford University Press, UK; USA and Canada Hope Publishing Co. © words Oxford University Press, UK, reprinted by permission.

Page 84: *The peace,* prayer for unity, Roman Missal.

Page 85: *La ténèbre n'est point ténèbre,* composer J. Berthier, "Chants de Taizé", No. 10, 1986 © Ateliers et Presses de Taizé, 71250 Cluny, France.

Page 86: *A litany of commandments,* from The Alternative Service Book 1980, Church of England, copyright © The Central Board of Finance of the Church of England 1980.

Pages 86 and 88: *Lord, have mercy upon us, and incline our hearts to keep this law,* and *Lord have mercy upon us, and write all these thy laws in our hearts, we beseech thee,* music John Merbecke (c.1550), arranged (1961), organ accompaniment by Healey Willan, adapted to the words of the Canadian Prayer Book, revised 1938 © The General Synod of the Anglican Church of Canada, "The Book of Common Praise", No. 179.

Page 89: *Kyrie Eleison 1,* mixed voices, "Music from Taizé", by Jacques Berthier, 1981 GIA Publications, © Ateliers et Presses de Taizé, 71250 Cluny, France; also: GIA Chicago; Collins Lit. Publ., London; Mowbrays, London.

O Lord hear my pray'r, 4 voices, composer J. Berthier, "Canons, litanies et répons de Taizé 5. Chants Nouveaux", 1982 © Ateliers et Presses de Taizé; also: GIA, Chicago; Collins Lit. Publ., London; Mowbrays, London.

Pages 89-92: *Two forms of intercession,* based on the Universal Declaration of Human Rights, by Thomas Hartley Dorris, World Council of Churches, Geneva, Switzerland.

Page 92: *Lord, we are your servants, your chosen ones,* prayer for ourselves as instruments of justice based on Isaiah 42 and 58. Source untraced.

O God, send us out into the world in peace. Source unknown.

Page 93: *Komm, Herr, segne uns/Bless and keep us, Lord,* © music and German text: Burckhardthaus-Laetere; English: Fred Kaan. Used with permission.

Page 94: *The time is coming, indeed, it is here,* Terry C. Falla, from "Be Our Freedom Lord". Source untraced.

Page 95: *Jesus, where can we find you,* © music and English text: Doreen Potter; used with the permission of WCC Publications; French: Etienne de Peyer; German: Reinhild Traitler.

Page 96: *Eternal God, you are the author of life.* Source unknown.

Eternal God, free us from fear and prejudice. Source unknown.

Page 97: *Litany of gratitude,* adapted from "New World Liturgy", Yohan Devananda, Sri Lanka.

Page 98: *Let us pray for all religious communities.* Source unknown.

Lord, make us instruments of your peace, traditionally by St Francis of Assisi.

Page 99: *Make me a channel of your peace,* words: traditional; music: Sebastian Temple; arrangement: DN; from "Songs for a Gospel", 1987 Wood Lake Books, Winfield, Canada, © Franciscan Communications, Los Angeles, California, USA. Reprinted with permission.

Page 101: *Lead us from death to life,* prayer for peace, Week of Prayer for World Peace, 1981, London, UK.

Page 102: *Affirmation of baptism,* renunciation of evil, profession of faith, and commitment to our baptismal covenant are adapted from the affirmation of baptism, Formular of the Lutheran Book of Worship, pp.199f., 1978 Ausgburg Publishing House, Philadelphia, USA.

Page 103: *Many are the lightbeams,* text original Swedish: Anders Frostenson; English: David Lewis; German: Burckhardthaus-Laetere Verlag, Offenbach; Spanish: Pablo Sosa; music: Olle Widestrand. © Music: Olle Widestrand. Used with permission.

Page 104: *Glory be to God the Father!,* "Lutheran Book of Worship", No. 167, 1978 Augsburg Publishing House, Philadelphia, USA.

Lord, our God, in baptism, Hans-Georg Link, Federal Republic of Germany.

Kyrie eleison, Orthodox liturgy, USSR.

Page 105: *Creator Spirit, who in the beginning.* Source unknown.

Page 106: *Agios o Theos,* Russian Orthodoxy liturgy.

Those who have been baptized in Christ, 1977 2nd edition "The Divine Liturgy of St John Chrysostom Hymnal", 1977 2nd ed. © Greek Orthodox Archdiocese of North and South America, Brookline, Massachusetts, USA. Reprinted with permission.

Page 107: *Water is an element of life and death,* Hans-Georg Link, Federal Republic of Germany.

Alleluia, Melchior Vulpius 1609.

Page 110: *Amen,* "The Book of Praise" (p.614), revised 1972 Presbyterian Church in Canada.

Page 111: *Laudate omnes gentes,* mixed voices, "Music from Taizé", by Jacques Berthier, 1981 GIA Publications, © Ateliers et Presses de Taizé 71250 Cluny, France; also: GIA, Chicago; Collins Lit. Publ., London: Mowbrays, London.

Page 112: *Lord, our God, we ask you for the strength,* Hans-Georg Link, Federal Republic of Germany.

Hear our prayer O Lord, by Terry MacArthur, USA, written for "With all God's People".

Appendix

1. *We Believe: Marantha the Light of the Day,* in "Report of the 1987 Asian Workshop on Liturgy and Music" (p.207), music: Francisco F. Feliciano, © Asian Institute for Liturgy and Music Publications, Manila, Philippines.

2. *Kyrie eleison,* Russian Orthodox.

3. *Chuyo chuyo turo chusoso,* in "Report of the 1987 Asian Workshop on Liturgy and Music" (p.109), © Ateliers et Presses de Taizé, 71250 Cluny, France.

4. *Senhor, tem piedade nós,* words and music by Jaci C. Maraschin, in "O Novo Canto da Terra" edited by Jaci C. Maraschin, No. 81, 1987 © Editora do Instituto Anglicano de Estudios Teológicos, Sao Paulo, Brazil.

5. *Aleluya,* Honduras. Source unknown.

6. *Wa Wa Emiwamimo,* in "African Songs of Worship", edited by I-to-Loh, 1986 © Renewal and Congregational Life, World Council of Churches Publications, Geneva, Switzerland.

7. *Vesnica pomenire,* "Cante de Cintari Bisericesti" (p.146), 1975 © Editura Institutului Biblic Si Misiune Ortodoxa, Bucharest, Romania.

8. *Jesu Tawa Pano (Jesus, we are here),* by Patrick Matsikenyiri, Cashel, Zimbabwe.

9. *Salamun,* Lebanon. Source unknown.

10. *Doamnemiluieste* (first 2 lines), "Cante de Cintari Bisericesti", (p.146), 1975 © Editura Institutului Biblic Si Misiune Ortodoxa, Bucharest, Romania.

11. *Porque El venció en la muerte la conjura de las malignas fuerzas de la historia,* text: Federico J. Pagura, music: Homero R. Perera, "Cancionero Abierto", 1982 © ISEDET, Buenos Aires, Argentina.